THE QUIT RENTS
OF VIRGINIA,
1704

Compiled by

Annie Laurie Wright Smith

Baltimore
GENEALOGICAL PUBLISHING CO., INC.
1987

Originally published: Richmond, Virginia, 1957
Reprinted: Genealogical Publishing Co., Inc.
Baltimore, 1975, 1977, 1980, 1987
Library of Congress Catalogue Card Number 75-7833
International Standard Book Number 0-8063-0674-2
Made in the United States of America

The Quit Rents of Virginia

Copy of the Rent Rolls of the Sevll
Countys in Virg^a for the year 1704
    referred to in Col. Nicholsons
    Lre: of the 25th July last.

    Recd: 8   October
    Read   1705
           M. 61

    Entred C: fol   365

           and
Land owners of that section called the
Northern Neck. No Quit Rents exist.

Preface

The Quit Rents of Virginia is in two parts. The first is the Quit Rent Roll of 1704 that includes the fourteen counties that paid their tribute to the King. It is the only one that survived the years. The Original is in the British Public Record Office, and a handwritten transcript is in the Library of Congress, Washington, D. C.

The second part of the Quit Rents of Virginia gives the five counties in the section of the state known as The Northern Neck. Their quit rents were paid to the Lords Proprietors, the Fairfax-Culpepper family. None of these records are in existence, but the names of the land owners are in the land grants of that period.

Sheriffs of 1704 in Virginia

Accomack Co.........	John Wise
Charles City Co	Thomas Parker
Elizabeth City Co	Henry Royall
Essex Co	Richard Covington
Gloucester Co	Thomas Neale and Ambrose Dudley
Henrico Co...........	
Isle of Wight Co	William Bridger
James City Co	Henry Soane junr
King and Queen Co	Robert Bird
King William Co......	
Middlesex Co	
Nansemond Co	Henry Jenkins
New Kent Co	James Mosse
Norfolk Co...........	James Wilson
Northampton Co	
Princess Anne Co	Henry Spratt
Prince George Co	Will Epes
Surry Co.............	Joseph John Jackman
Warwick Co..........	Robert Hubbard
York Co	William Barber

The College of William and Mary was obliged by its charter to pay two copies of Latin verses to the Governour every fifth of November as quit rents for its land.

W & M vol. 16 p 15

Until the reign of Queen Anne the English Language was extremely variable and unsettled. The best informed men, writing of the same period, would spell the same words very differently. (see Quit Rents for variations in names) Preface to Henings pxi

The Laws of Virginia

At a Grand Assembly   Charles I King
6th January 1639-40
                                       Sir Frances Wyatt Gov
Act xxiv
    Seven years after date of patents 2s. per hundred acres quit
rents to be paid yearly at some convienent place to be appointed in
each county.

                                       Henings Statutes, I, 228

At a Grand Assembly   Charles I King
Holden at James City, 2nd March 1642-43
                        Sir William Berkeley, Knight, Governor
Act Lxxii
    Whereas it was enacted at an Assembly in January 1640 in
explanation of the time when quit rents vpon grants of land are due,
That all those grants that were of seaven years continuance or above
were to beginn their payments. Their first years payment at the
feast of St. Michael the Archangel 1639 and soe forwards and that
all other grants should have the benefit to be free from quit rents
vntil seaven years after their first grant, which is enacted and con-
firmed by this present Grand Assembly.

                                       Henings Statutes, I, 280

At a Grand Assembly
Holden at James City, 20th November 1645
                        Sir William Berkeley, Knight, Governour
Act xvii
    According to his majesties gracious bounty to this collony ex-
pressed in his late Royal letters, Be it enacted by the Governour,
Council and Burgesses of this Grand Assembly that all the quit rents
for land due to his Majestie in this colloney be disposed of as followeth,
first allowing to the treasurer for the time being his salary of £500 per
ann. as the revenues shall amount thereto, and then what shall arise
by surplussage the accompt thereof to be presented to the Governor
and Council and then to be disposed of by the Assembly as they think fit.

                                       Henings Statutes, I, 306

Second Session, March 1645-6
Act xiv
    Be it enacted by this present Grand Assembly, That his Ma'ties
treasurer do receive the Quit Rents in Tobacco at the rate of 3d. per
pound. It being conceived the value of the comoditie at present.

                                       Henings Statutes, I, 316

Act xx
  Whereas there is and has been great neglect in the payment of
quitt rents vpon the motion of the treasurer, for remedy thereof, Bee
it enacted and declared as followeth, That the delinquents in the payment of any quit rents shall be destranyed vpon the lands by the treas-
urers receivers by direction and warrent from vnder his hand, And
that if any will repleavy their goods, then giving good good caution,
their allegations shall be heard, either at the countie courts or
before the Governour and Council, And the Kings suits and debts be
preferred any other, And that all courts and officers ought to be
assistant therein and proceed according to the laws of England.

Hening Statutes, I, 351

At a General Assembly
Begun and Holden at
The Capitol in the city of Williamsburg, on the second day of
November, in the seventh year of the reign of our sovereign Lord
George the first, by the grace of God, of Great Britain, France and
Ireland, King, defender of the faithetc, and in the year of our lord 1720.

Chapter ii
  Every sheriff at November court yearly is to divide his county
into precincts, appoint and publickly, one place in each precinct, --set
the time of his appearance there before February 20th annually, To
these places the people are to bring their quit rents either in current
money or in tobacco at one penny per pound. If the sheriff dont do the
people justice by these appointments the county courts are to direct
and order others. And if the people fail the sherriff makes distress
and sale for satisfaction of the quit rents, The sheriff or collector to
be answerable for all quit rents, if sufficient distress can be had vpon
the lands liable. To pay the sweet scented tobacco in hogsheads of
seven hundred nett, and the Aranoka six hundred nett, and paid vpon
demand. If the proprietor lives out of the county, the sherriff is to
notify the collector of the other county. And if the proprietor lives
out of the Collony, his attorney is to be notified, if none, then a
notice is to be put on outside of court house, - etc, Double quit rents
are levied against this property. All persons concealing any part of
his land shall pay double quit rents. For better discovery of such
persons, the moiety of such double quit rents is given to the person
discovering the concealment.

Henings Statutes, 4, 79

At a General Assembly
Begun and Held
At the Capitol, in the City of Williamsburg, on Monday 20th, Oct. 1777
2nd year of the Commonwealth, Patrick Henry, Governor
"Be it enacted that all lands within this Commonwealth shall
henceforth be exempted and discharged from the payments of all quit
rents, except the lands in that tract between Rappahannock and
Potomack rivers known as the Northern Neck.

Henings Statutes, 9, 359

------- A -------

		Acres
Allen Reynold.	New Kent Co?	205
Allen Richard	" " "	550
Allen Robert	" " "	100
Allen Samuel	" " "	150
Allen Thomas	Accomack Co	700
Allen Thomas	Isle of Wight Co	150
Allen William.	York Co	117
Alligood Henry	Northampton Co	100
Alligood John	" "	300
Allin Edmd..	Accomack Co	200
Allin Erasmus	Essex Co	100
Allin Richard	Middlesex Co	150
Allin Thomas	Elizabeth City Co	227
Allin Thomas	King & Queen Co	100
Allin Widdo	Henrico Co	99
Allin William	Essex Co	100
Alvis George	New Kent Co	325
Ally Henry	Prince George Co	390
Alvey Robert	King William Co	400
Ambrose Leonard	Ware-Gloucester Co	200
Ames Joseph	Accomack Co	375
Amis James.	Petso-Gloucester Co	250
Amos Fran.	New Kent Co	100
Amos Nicho.	" " "	50
Anderson Charles Mr.	Prince George Co	505
Anderson Henry	" " "	250
Anderson John.	" " "	228
Anderson Matt	" " "	349
Anderson Tho.	" " "	450
Anderson Wm..	" " "	235
Anderson David	New Kent Co	300
Anderson John	" " "	100
Anderson John	" " "	100
Anderson Richard	" " "	200
Anderson Robert	" " "	700
Anderson Robert	" " "	900
Anderson George	Isle of Wight Co	150
Anderson John	York Co	50
Anderson Richard	King & Queen Co	650
Anderson Wm. Capt	King William Co	150
Andrews Andrew	Northampton Co	100
Andrews Bartho.	Surry Co	375
Andrews David	" "	225
Andrews George	Essex Co	200
Andrews John	Kingston-Gloucester Co	50
Andrews Robert	Northampton Co	300
Andrews Robert	Tax due Accomack Co	500
Andrews Robert	Surry Co	130
Andrews Thomas	" "	190
Andrews Thomas	Henrico Co	396
Andrews Wm..	King William Co	100
Andrews Wm.	Accomack Co	300
Andros Henry.	York Co	274
Angell James	Northampton Co	100
Anguish Patrick	Princess Anne Co	150
Anniers Elizabeth	Ware-Gloucester Co	250

		Acres
Anthony Mark	New Kent Co	190
Anthony George	Accomack Co	100
Aperson William	James City Co	80
Applewaite Henry	Isle of Wight Co	1500
Arcade Mr. Welburn	Accomack Co	1854
Archer Elizabeth	York Co	370
Archer George	Henrico Co	1738
Archer Jno.	" "	335
Archer Stephen	Nansemond Co	200
Archer by Tho. Nobbling	Elizabeth City Co	212
Arew Jno.	Accomack Co	234
Argo James	James City Co	200
Arise Margt.	New Kent Co	200
Arlin Jeremiah	Nansemond Co	250
Armestone Joshua	James City Co	50
Armistead Coll. Anthony	Elizabeth City Co	2140
Armistead Maj. Wm.	" " "	460
Armistead Capt. Wm.	Middlesex Co	2325
Armistead Capt.	Kingston-Gloucester Co	3675
Armistead Wm.	Kingston-Gloucester Co	300
Armistead Wm.	Ware-Gloucester Co	100
Armistead William	Petso-Gloucester Co	430
Armsby John	King William Co	200
Armtrading Henry.	Accomack Co	175
Arnold Anthony	King William Co	100
Arnold Benj.	" " "	1000
Arnold Edward	Nansemond Co	80
Arnold Edward	King & Queen Co	150
Aron Josiah	New Kent Co	200
Arving Wm.	Essex Co	100
Asban by John Collins	Accomack Co	1666
Asbrook Peter senr.	Henrico Co	200
Ascoutch Mary	" "	633
Ascow Thomas	Warwick Co	50
Ashby William	Princess Anne Co	100
Ashcroft Thomas	New Kent Co	180
Ashley Charles	" " "	100
Ashley Dennis	Norfolk Co	150
Askew John	Isle of Wight Co	100
Askew Nicholas	" " " "	80
Asque John	King & Queen Co	320
Atkin James sr	Henrico Co tax due	32
Atkins Jane	Isle of Wight Co	600
Atkins John	" " " "	200
Atkins Thomas	Surry Co	80
Atkinson James	Isle of Wight Co	400
Atkinson John	New Kent Co	300
Atkinson Richd.	Surry Co	100
Atwell Thomas	Nansemond Co.	440
Attwood Edward	Princess Anne Co	400
Atwood Richard	Middlesex Co	100
Austin Danll	King & Queen Co	80
Austin James	New Kent Co	700
Austin-----	" " "	245
Austin Johanna	Abbington-Gloucester Co	40
Austin Richard	New Kent Co	50

4

		Acres
Austin Thomas	King & Queen Co	100
Averett John	Surry Co	120
Avery John	" "	150
Avery John	Prince George Co	100
Avis Widdow	Norfolk Co	50
Aylsberry Phillip	Nansemond Co	100
Aylworth Jona	Accomack Co	200
Ayres William	Essex Co	200
Ayres Edmund	Accomack Co	1000
Ayres Frances	" "	300
Ayres Henry	" "	250
Ayres Ragnall	" "	300

------- B -------

Babb John	Nansemond Co	500
Babb Thom. per Selden	Elizabeth City Co	300
Babb Widdow	Abbington-Gloucester Co	150
Babington Thomas	Norfolk Co	150
Bacheldon Joseph	" "	300
Bacon John	Kingston-Gloucester Co	825
Bacop Thomas	Ware-Gloucester Co	200
Bad Samuell	New Kent Co	150
Badger Reynold	Accomack Co	150
Bagby Robert	King & Queen Co	550
Bagby Thomas	James City Co	180
Baggally Gervis	Accomack Co	700
Bagley Edward	Surry Co	350
Bagley Peter	Surry Co	100
Bagwell Alex.	Accomack Co	413
Bagwell Edward	" "	200
Bagwell Henry	" "	412
Bagwell John	" "	465
Bagwell Thomas	" "	465
Baile John	Surry Co	250
Bailer John	Essex Co	800
Bailey Richard	Petso-Gloucester Co	600
Bailey Richard	Ware-Gloucester Co	800
Bailey Thomas	Henrico Co	251
Baines Thomas	Elizabeth City Co	50
Baites Isaac	Prince George Co	360
Baker Christe	New Kent Co	100
Baker Coll Henry	Surry Co	850
Baker Henry	Essex Co	350
Baker Henry	Nansemond Co	375
Baker Henry	Isle of Wight Co	750
Baker James	King & Queen Co	322
Baker James	Elizabeth City Co	225
Baker John	Accomack Co	400
Baker John	King William Co	250

		Acres
Baker John	Northampton Co	400
Baker John	New Kent Co	130
Baker John	James City Co	100
Baker Joseph	Nansemond Co	740
Baker Ralph	Petso-Gloucester Co	150
Baker Richard	New Kent Co	80
Baker Richard	Nansemond Co	40
Baker Robert	" "	50
Baker Sarah	Surry Co	50
Baker Thomas	King William Co	100
Baker William	King & Queen Co	350
Balingtine Alexander	Norfolk Co	300
Balingtine George	" "	510
Balingtine William	" "	60
Balington John	" "	150
Balington Richard	" "	50
Ball David	New Kent Co	200
Ball John	Essex Co	150
Ballard Elizabeth	Nansemond Co	300
Ballard Mr. Francis	Elizabeth City Co	460
Ballard John	Nansemond Co	400
Ballard Joseph	" "	200
Ballard Thomas	James City Co	100
Ballard William	" " "	300
Ballis Widdow	Elizabeth City Co	350
Bally Charles	Accomack Co	929
Bally Edmund	" "	800
Bally Edward	" "	300
Bally John	" "	1000
Bally Richard senr	" "	2100
Bally Richard junr	" "	180
Bally Robert	" "	100
Banister Mr John orphans	Prince George Co, tax due	1970
Banister John	Kingston-Gloucester Co	650
Banister John	Abbington-Gloucester Co	2750
Banks Andrew	New Kent Co	50
Banks William	King & Queen Co	1079
Banyman Alex	York Co	50
Baptist Morgan	" "	100
Barbee William	Middlesex Co	150
Barber James	King & Queen Co	750
Barber Thomas	New Kent Co	500
Barber Thomas	York Co	600
Bardin John	Isle of Wight Co	100
Barefield John	Nansemond Co	300
Barefield Richard	" "	900
Barefield Thomas	" "	100
Barington William	Norfolk Co	100
Barker Charles	New Kent Co	100
Barker Jery	Surry Co	420
Barker John	" "	1160
Barlowe George	Isle of Wight Co	80
Barlow Henry	King & Queen Co	200
Barlow John	Prince George Co	50
Barlow Robert	Abbington-Gloucester Co	62
Barrnes Anthony	Princess Anne Co	200

		Acres
Barnes Francis	James City Co	200
Barnes Henry	Middlesex Co	200
Barnes John	Isle of Wight Co	
Barnhowes Richd.	New Kent Co	1600
Barnoe Lewis	York Co	80
Barratt Wm.	James City Co	305
Barrett Christo.	New Kent Co	60
Barron Andrew	Essex Co	50
Barron Tho.	James City Co	100
Baron James	Isle of Wight	300
Bartee Robert	Norfolk Co	150
Barter Joell	Surry Co	100
Bartholomew Charles	Prince George Co	600
Bartlett Tho.	Essex Co	100
Barton Andrew	King & Queen Co	150
Baskett John	" " "	150
Baskett Esqr Wm.	New Kent Co	1250
Baskewyle Geo.	York Co	350
Basnett John	Princess Anne Co	250
Bassett Coll.	King William Co	1550
Bassett Tho.	New Kent Co	350
Bassett Wm. Esqr	" " "	4100
Bassett Wm	" " "	550
Bates Alice	Ware-Gloucester Co	200
Bates Edwd	New Kent Co	50
Bates Capt Henry orphans	Prince George Co tax due	1200
and mother Mrs Mary Bates. . . .		
Bates James	York Co	117
Bates Jno.	" "	669
Bateson-----	Northampton Co	200
Bathurst Edward	Nansemond Co	250
Batthurst Coll. Lemuel	New Kent Co tax due	800
Batt Henry	Prince George Co	790
Batt Wm.	" " "	750
Battail John	Essex Co	1100
Battaile Wm.	Nansemond Co	800
Batten George	Princess Anne Co	150
Batterton Tho.	King & Queen Co	100
Baugh James	Henrico Co	458
Baugh John	" "	448
Baughan Henry	Essex Co	100
Baughan James senr	" "	600
Baughan James	" "	150
Baughan John	New Kent Co	100
Baughan John jr	" " "	300
Baughan Joseph	" " "	100
Baulwar James	Essex Co	800
Baulwar James	" "	200
Baulwar John	" "	50
Baugtwright Jno.	New Kent Co	250
Baxter James	New Kent Co	90
Baxter John	Charles City Co	250
Bayley Abr.	Henrico Co	542
Bayley Jno.	Elizabeth City Co	415
Bayley Jno.	New Kent Co	80
Bayley Walter	Norfolk Co	290

		Acres
Bayley Wm.	James City Co	100
Baylor John	King & Queen Co	3000
Beach Sarah	Accomack Co	300
Beadwine John	Northampton Co	200
Beamond Edw.	Nansemond Co	550
Bear Peter	New Kent Co	100
Bear Joseph	" " "	150
Beard Richd	Kingston-Gloucester Co	380
Beard Wm.	" " "	100
Bearne Henry	New Kent Co	50
Beck Andrew	Prince George Co	300
Beck Wm.	New Kent Co	433
Beck Wm. Mr	" " "	200
Beck Wm. Mr	King William Co tax due	1600
Beckham Symon	Essex Co	100
Beckitt Tho.	James City Co	60
Bedford Thomas	Kingston-Gloucester Co	50
Bedingfield Theo	Charles City Co	110
Beesley Wm	Essex Co	100
Beeswell Robert	" "	100
Beeswell Robert jr	" "	150
Bell Andrew	Kingston-Gloucester Co	128
Bell Edwds	King William Co	580
Bell Edwd	Accomack Co	101
Bell George	Elizabeth City Co	80
Bell George	Northampton Co	400
Bell John	Isle of Wight	200
Bell Jno	Surry Co	180
Bell Robert	Accomack Co	650
Bell Roger	King & Queen Co	150
Bell Tho. senr	Accomack Co	100
Bell Tho. junr	" "	100
Bell Thomas	Essex Co	100
Belson Jane	Nansemond Co	100
Benbridge Geo.	Surry Co	200
Bendall John	Essex Co	135
Bendry Widdo	" "	700
Benford James	Prince George Co	461
Benge Robert	James City Co	60
Benham John	" " "	50
Benjafield Jos.	York Co	80
Benn Mary	Isle of Wight	675
Bennees Mr Thom. orphans	Surry Co	950
-Mr Thom. Holt refuses to pay tax.		
Bennett Alexander	King & Queen Co	200
Bennett James	Surry Co	200
Bennett John	?????ownsin Norfolk Co	33
Bennett Richard	Isle of Wight Co	70
Benett Richd	Surry Co	200
Bennett Sawyer	King & Queen Co	150
Bennett William	" " "	150
Benson Thomas	Princess Anne Co	225
Benson Wm. junr	Accomack Co	270
Benstone Alex.	" "	270
Benstone Francis	" "	400
Benstone Rebeckha	" "	270

		Acres
Benstone Samuel	Accomack Co	300
Benthall Danll	Northampton Co	258
Benthall Joseph senr	" "	793
Benthall Joseph junr	" "	150
Bentley --------	Surry Co	180
Benton Francis	Nansemond Co	200
Bentley John	James City Co	125
Benton Epaphra	Nansemond Co	250
Benton John	" "	660
Benules Mr Tho. orphans held by Capt Thom. Holt	Surry Co	950
Berham Robt.	Surry Co	650
Berkeley Capt.	Middlesex Co	750
Bernard Samuel	Petso-Gloucester Co	550
Bernard William	" " "	810
Bernes John senr.	Accomack Co	657
Berry Patrick	Kingston-Gloucester Co	250
Berry Robert	?????landin Norfolk Co	95
Berry William	Richmond Co tax due	400
Berwick George	Middlesex Co	100
Best Edmund	James City Co	75
Best Thomas	Nansemond Co	160
Best William	Isle of Wight Co	100
Bevan Thomas	" " " "	100
Bevell Essex	Henrico Co	200
Bevill John	" "	495
Beven Wm	Accomack Co	400
Beverly Harry	Essex Co	1000
Beverley Harry	Middlesex Co	1000
Beverley Harry	King William Co tax due	1000
Beverley Majr Peter	Ware-Gloucester	800
Beverley Mr Robert	Elizabeth City Co	777
Beverly Robt	Henrico Co	988
Beverley Robt	King & Queen Co	3000
Bibb Benj.	King William Co	100
Bickley Joseph	" " "	150
Bigg Thomas	Norfolk Co	100
Biggins Arthur	Prince George Co	200
Bighton Richd	Surry Co	590
Bill Robert	King & Queen Co	150
Billington Mary	Essex Co	200
Billot Jno	Northampton Co	400
Billott Wm	" "	100
Billups George	Kingston-Gloucester Co	1200
Bimms Christo	James City Co	300
Bincham Jno	Surry Co	100
Bine Edmund	King & Queen Co	111
Bineham James	Surry Co	157
Bingley James	James City Co	100
Birchett Edward	Prince George Co	886
Birchett Robt	" " "	375
Bird Robert	King & Queen Co	1324
Bird Widdo	Essex Co	100
Bird Majr. Wm	King William Co	1200
Bird William	King & Queen Co	572
Bishop John senr	Prince George Co	100

Acres

Bishop John junr	Prince George Co	100
Bishop Robt	Charles City Co	200
Bishop Wm.	Norfolk Co	100
Biswell Thomas	Nansemond Co	400
Black George	James City Co	200
Blackbourne Capt	Abbington-Gloucester Co	550
Blackburn Rowland	New Kent Co	700
Blackbun Wm	Surry Co	150
Blackiston Argail	Essex Co	200
Blackistone Thomas	Warwick Co	75
Blackley Robt	Middlesex Co	100
Blackley Wm	James City Co	142
Blackman Wm	Henrico Co	175
Blackson John	Northampton Co	100
Blackwell James	New Kent Co	950
Blackwell James jr	" " "	200
Blackwell Wm and Wm. Burrows	own in New Kent Co	
	own in Henrico Co	63
Blaiss Mrs	Middlesex Co	300
Blake Anne Widdo	Accomack Co	120
Blake Arthur	Norfolk Co	200
Blake Elias	Accomack Co	430
Blake John	" "	310
Blake George	Middlesex Co	100
Blake Wm	Surry Co	200
Blake Wm	King & Queen Co	290
Blake Wm junr	" " "	210
Blakey Thomas	Middlesex Co	100
Blalock Jno	New Kent Co	492
Blanch Wm	Norfolk Co	100
Blanchard Benj	Nansemond Co	130
Blanchet John	King & Queen Co	125
Bland Henry	" " "	150
Bland Richard	Prince George Co	1000
Bland Sarah	Surry Co	1455
Blankitt Henry	James City Co	100
Blanks Henry	" " "	650
Blanks Richard senr	Charles City Co	250
Blanks Richard junr	" " "	125
Blanks Thomas	" " "	125
Blessington John	Nansemond Co	150
Blewford Thomas	Middlesex Co	100
Blico Christo	Surry Co	50
Blitchodin Tho	Prince George Co	284
Blocksom John	Accomack Co	700
Blumpton Henry	Nansemond Co	1500
Blunt Thomas	Surry Co	1355
Bobo Elizabeth	King William Co	200
Bocus Reynold	King & Queen Co	150
Body Wm	Isle of Wight Co	1375
Bohannah Duncan	Kingston-Gloucester Co	113-1/2
Bohannah John	" " "	113-1/2
Bohannah Joseph	" " "	148
Boisseau James	King & Queen Co	900
Bolling Coll.	Prince George Co	3402
Bolling John	Henrico Co	831

		Acres
Bolling Robert	Henrico Co	500
Bolton Henry	Kingston-Gloucester Co	50
Bolton Richard	Norfolk Co	700
Bolton Wm	" "	212
Boman-----	James City Co	90
Bond Frances	Princess Anne Co	264
Bond John	King & Queen Co	100
Bond John	Nansemond Co	150
Bond Richard	" "	90
Bond William	Norfolk Co	200
Boner George	Northampton Co	150
Bonny Richard	Princess Anne Co	2000
Bonwell Thomas	Accomack Co	300
Booker Capt.	Abbington-Gloucester Co	1000
Booker Mary	Petso-Gloucester Co	100
Booker Richard	York Co	200
Booker Mr. Rvend	Elizabeth City Co	526
Bookey Edwd	Surry Co	180
Booth Jno	Accomack Co & Princess Anne	300
Booth Joseph	Nansemond Co	987
Booth Widdo	Essex Co	800
Borum Edwd	Kingston-Gloucester Co	360
Boseman Henry	Isle of Wight Co	160
Bostock Jno	New Kent Co	100
Bostock Wm	" " "	80
Boswell Dorothy	Ware-Gloucester Co	1600
Boswell Joseph	" " "	230
Boswell Wm	Elizabeth City Co	220
Botman Harmon	Charles City Co	100
Bottom John	Henrico Co	100
Bougher Phill	Surry Co	100
Boules Tho.	Accomack Co	300
Boulmer Tho.	York Co	265
Boult Roger	" "	100
Bourn John	Essex Co	100
Bourne Andrew	Nansemond Co	200
Bourne George	King & Queen Co	200
Bourn William	New Kent Co	140
Bow Henry	" " "	200
Bowden Tho	King & Queen Co	150
Bowers Arthur	Essex Co	600
Bowers John	Norfolk Co	166
Bower Wm	James City Co	50
Bowes Henry	Nansemond Co	600
Bowger John	Warwick Co	100
Bowker Ralph	King & Queen Co	330
Bowles Henry	Norfolk Co	330
Bowles John	New Kent Co	500
Bowles John	Elizabeth City Co	260
Bowles Robt	King & Queen Co	100
Bowman Edwd	Henrico Co	300
Bowman John jr	" "	300
Bowman Len	" "	65
Bowman Peter	Essex Co	400
Boykin Edward	Isle of Wight Co	1100

		Acres
Boyne Epapap	Nansemond Co	100
Boyt Thomas	" "	400
Bracey Hugh	Isle of Wight Co	1000
Bracey Wm	Warwick Co	150
Brackitt Tho	James City Co	150
Bradburn Richd	Essex Co	100
Bradbury George	New Kent Co	100
Bradford John	Accomack Co	364
Bradford Richd	Charles City Co	1397
Bradford Wm	Accomack Co	3500
Bradingham Robert	New Kent Co	150
Bradley Henry	Nansemond Co	500
Bradley Joseph	Charles City Co	200
Bradley Richard	Nansemond Co	250
Bradley Thomas	New Kent Co	255
Brady Joseph	Nansemond Co	250
Bragg James	Isle of Wight Co	500
Braisseur Mr John	Nansemond Co	400
Bramble Henry	Norfolk Co	100
Branch Benjamin	Henrico Co	550
Branch Christo	" "	646
Branch Francis	Isle of Wight Co	50
Branch James	Henrico Co	555
Branch John	Isle of Wight Co	45
Branch Matthew	Henrico Co	947
Branch Thomas	" "	540
Brand Richard	James City Co	125
Branson ffrancis	Northampton Co	100
Brantley Edward	Isle of Wight Co	175
Brantley John	" " " "	364
Branton John	Norfolk Co	330
Braseal Henry	Henrico Co	200
Brasur John	Essex Co	300
Braswell Richard	Isle of Wight Co	100
Bratley Ph.	" " " "	200
Braxton George	King & Queen Co	2825
Bray Anne	Ware-Gloucester Co	100
Bray Capt Bloomer	Princess Anne Co	270
Bray David	James City Co	5758
Bray David Tax due in	King William Co	1000
Bray David	Charles City Co	230
Bray James	King William Co	1400
Bray James	James City Co	3500
Bray John	King & Queen Co	230
Bray Sarah	New Kent Co	790
Bray Heirsof	" " tax due	500
Bray of Warwick Co has small track in Surrey tax due		
Brazeal Henry jr	Henrico Co	300
Breeding George	King & Queen Co	200
Breeding John	James City Co	100
Breeding John	New Kent Co	300
Breemer John	King & Queen Co	1100
Breemer John jr	" " " "	200
Breltven Mich.	Elizabeth City Co	100
Brewer John	Northampton Co	50
Brewer Mary	New Kent Co	100

12

		Acres
Brewer Nicho	Prince George Co	100
Brewer Robert	Nansemond Co	200
Brewer Thomas	Isle of Wight Co	200
Briberry John	Princess Anne Co	50
Brice Henry	Essex Co	400
Brickhouse Geo	Northampton Co	2100
Bridgate John in England	Essex Co tax due	700
Bridgeforth James	King & Queen Co	355
Bridger Joseph.	Isle of Wight Co	580
Bridger Col. Samuel	Nansemond Co	500
Bridger Samuell	Isle of Wight Co	200
Bridger Wm. & Saml	" " " "	12900
Bridgwater Samll	Henrico Co	280
Bridle Francis	Isle of Wight Co	250
Brigs Charles	Surry Co	331
Brigs Henry	Surry Co	100
Briggs James	Isle of Wight Co	100
Briggs John	Princess Anne Co	600
Briggs Samll	Surry Co	300
Briggs Sarah	" "	300
Bright Robt. senr	Elizabeth City Co	100
Brightwell Elizb	King William Co	300
Brinkley John	Nansemond Co	430
Brinkley Michael	" "	200
Brinson Matth.	Princess Anne Co	250
Briston Jacob	Middlesex Co	100
Bristow John	" "	140
Bristow Robt. Esqr	Ware-Gloucester Co	2050
Bristow Robt. Esqr Tax paid . .	Kingston-Gloucester Co	900
Britt John	Isle of Wight Co	350
Britt Wm	Nansemond Co	400
Brittingham Wm	Accomack Co	538
Brittler Matus	Prince George Co	510
Broach John	King & Queen Co	1200
Broadbent Joshua	Abbington-Gloucester Co	200
Broadhurst Capt John	Accomack Co	1100
Broadnax Jno. J	Henrico Co	725
Broadnax Wm	James City Co	1683
Broadwater Wm	Accomack Co	500
Broch Robert	Isle of Wight Co	400
Brock Thomas	Princess Anne Co	400
Brock Wm	" " "	100
Bromell Peter	Middlesex Co	100
Brooken Martha	Petso-Gloucester Co	600
Brookins------	Essex Co	250
Brooks James	" "	100
Brooks. Jane of Henrico 6n 550 acres owned by Wm. Walker, New Kent.		
Brooks Jeane	Northampton Co	100
Brooks Job	Princess Anne Co	150
Brooks John	" " "	100
Brooks Joseph	Kingston-Gloucester Co	500
Brooks Peter	Essex Co	275
Brooks Richard	New Kent Co	85
Brooks Robert	Essex Co	400
Brooks Robert	" "	150
Brooks Robert	New Kent Co	45

		Acres
Brooks Robert	Charles City Co	150
Brooks Wm.	Kingston-Gloucester Co	720
Brothers Jno	New Kent Co	200
Brothers John	Nansemond Co	460
Brotherton Edwd	Accomack Co	600
Browder Edmd	Prince George Co	100
Brown Andrew	Nansemond Co	25
Brown Buskinhan	Essex Co	400
Brown Charles	Essex Co	1000
Brown Danll senr	" "	450
Brown Danll junr	" "	150
Brown Edward	Norfolk Co	300
Brown ffrancis	Essex Co	150
Brown James	James City Co	250
Brown Tho : Blakes land	King & Queen Co	300
Brown John	New Kent Co	100
Brown Lancelet	King & Queen Co	385
Brown Marmaduke	Charles City Co	100
Brown Martha	Henrico Co	893
Brown Thomas	Northampton Co	1862
Brown Thomas	Essex Co	50
Brown Widdo	Norfolk Co	270
Brown Wm.	" "	100
Brown Wm.	Essex Co	420
Brown Wm.	Isle of Wight Co	150
Browne Abraham	King William Co	250
Browne Doctor	Princess Anne Co	600
Browne Edwd	Surry Co	200
Browne George	York Co	150
Browne James	Warwick Co	150
Browne John	Surry Co	600
Browne John	Isle of Wight Co	100
Browne Joseph	King William Co	270
Browne Coll. Wm	Surry Co	2510
Browne Capt. Wm	" "	398
Browne William	James City Co	1070
Browne Wm	York Co	200
Bruce Abraham	Norfolk Co	1010
Bruce John	" "	300
Bruer Shackfield	James City Co	350
Bruin William	Nansemond Co	300
Brukins------	Essex Co	250
Brumley Wm.	Kingston-Gloucester	750
Brush Richard	Essex Co	250
Brutnall Richd	" "	100
Bruton James	Surry Co	500
Bruton Parish Gleabe	York Co	300
Bruxe Anne	Accomack Co	180
Bryan Charles	New Kent Co	100
Bryan James	Isle of Wight Co	1200
Bryan John	" " " "	200
Bryan John	Nansemond Co	200
Bryan Wm	Isle of Wight Co	200
Bryon John	James City Co	100
Bryon Lewis	Nansemond Co	400
Bryon William	" "	350

14

		Acres
Buck John	Princess Anne Co	250
Buck Thomas	York Co	350
Bucken Wm.	Norfolk Co	410
Buckner John	Ware-Gloucester Co	900
Buckner Richard	Essex Co	1200
Buckner Thomas	Petso-Gloucester Co	850
Buckner Thomas	Essex Co	2000
Buckner William	Gloucester owns Essex tax	1500
Buckner William	York Co	302
Bud Thomas	Accomack Co	500
Bugg Samll	New Kent Co	60
Bulkley Benj	" " "	200
Bull Henry	Norfolk Co	1500
Bull Robert sr	" "	1050
Bull Thomas	" "	2200
Bullard John	Ware-Gloucester Co	100
Bullington Benja	Henrico Co	100
Bullington John	" " 44 tax due	144
Bullington Robert	" "	100
Bullock Edward	New Kent Co	450
Bullock George	Northampton Co	100
Bullock George	Princess Anne Co	300
Bullock John	King & Queen Co	200
Bullock Mary	Surry Co	100
Bullock Richard	New Kent Co	450
Bullock Thomas	Isle of Wight Co	100
Bumpus Robert	New Kent Co	100
Bunch John	" " "	100
Bunch Paul	King William Co	150
Bundike Richd	Accomack Co	773
Bunell Hezichiah	Surry Co	150
Bunting Wm	Accomack Co	150
Burch Henry	King William Co	200
Burch John	King & Queen Co	100
Burch Wm.	" " "	100
Burford Wm.	" " "	150
Burges Edwd.	King William Co	150
Burges George	Norfolk Co	200
Burgess Robert	" "	535
Burgess Stephen	Warwick Co	128
Burgess Wm	King & Queen Co	100
Burgony John	Henrico Co	100
Burkett Tho.	New Kent Co	41
Burlowe Philip	Prince George Co	350
Burly Jno	New Kent Co	225
Burnell Edwd.	" " "	200
Burnell Mrs. Mary	" " "	2750
Burnett John	" " "	150
Burnett John	Essex Co	365
Burnett Tho. jr	" "	130
Burnett Tho. jr	" "	1000
Burnham Thomas	York Co	50
Burocke John	Accomack Co	200
Burrel Suprian	King William Co	350
Burroughs Mr. Benj	Princess Anne Co	800
Burroughs Wm.	" " "	50

		Acres
Burrows Wm & Wm Blackwell of New Kent Co own in Henrico		63
Burrus John	King William Co	60
Burrus Thomas	" " "	60
Burt Richard	York Co	200
Burton James	Ware-Gloucester Co	100
Burton George	Warwick Co	330
Burton Henry	Charles City Co	100
Burton Isaac	Henrico Co	100
Burton Ralph	James City Co	200
Burton Robert	Henrico Co	1350
Burton Tho.	Accomack Co	600
Burton Wm	" "	500
Burton Wm.	Henrico Co	294
Burwell Lewis	Charles City Co	8000
Burwell Lewis	York Co	2100
Burwell Lewis	James City Co	1350
Burwell Lewis	New Kent Co	200
Burwell Majr. Lewis	Isle of Wight Co	7000
Burwell Major	King William Co	4700
Burwell Major	Abbington-Gloucester Co	3300
Burwell Nathaniel	Ware-Gloucester Co	600
Busby Capt. Tho	Prince George Co	300
Busby Thomas	" " "	200
Bush John	James City Co	800
Bush Maj. Samuel	Norfolk Co	1628
Bush Mr. Samll	Princess Anne Co	550
Bushell Jno. jr	Elizabeth City Co	150
Butcher John	Essex Co	150
Butler Elizabeth	Nansemond Co	200
Butler James	" "	75
Butler John	" "	200
Butler John	Essex Co	125
Butler Jno.	" "	100
Butler John	Prince George Co	1385
Butler John	Abbington-Gloucester Co	100
Butler Thomas	King William Co	150
Butler William	Nansemond Co	120
Butler William	Prince George Co	283
Butt Richard	Norfolk Co	1840
Butts Alice	New Kent Co	150
Buttris Robert	King William Co	400
Buxton Samuell	James City Co	300
Byrd Esqr.	Henrico Co	19500
Byrd Coll. Esqr	Prince George Co	100
Byrd Wm.	Nansemond Co	300
Byrom Henry	Essex Co	100
Byron Robert	Abbington-Gloucester Co	400
Byron Roger	Norfolk Co	200

------- C -------

		Acres
Cahoone Samuel	Nansemond Co	240
Callaway Joseph	Essex Co	87
Callinet Jno	Northampton Co	100
Callis John	Kingston-Gloucester Co	1000
Calthorp James	York Co	900
Calvert Phil	Middlesex Co	200
Cambo Richd	New Kent Co	80
Cambridge ffrancis	Nansemond Co	100
Camell Hannah	Petso-Gloucester Co	100
Cammell Alexander	King & Queen Co	200
Camp Thomas	" " "	250
Camp William	Abbington-Gloucester Co	175
Campbell Alexander	Nansemond Co	500
Campbell John	" "	400
Campble Capt. Hugh	Princess Anne Co	800
Camoll Alexander	Isle of Wight Co	200
Candenscaine Obedience	Surry Co	200
Cane John	King & Queen Co	300
Cannon Edward	Princess Anne Co	550
Cannon John	Warwick Co	75
Cannon John	Henrico Co	108
Capell Tho	James City Co	200
Caple Nathaniel	Northampton Co	100
Capps Richard	Princess Anne Co	100
Capps William	Princess Anne Co	1050
Cardwell Tho.	Henrico Co	350
Carleton Anne	King & Queen Co	300
Carleton Christo	" " "	200
Carleton Jno	" " "	300
Carleton Tho	" " "	200
Carleton Wm	New Kent Co	140
Carley Richd	" " "	80
Carlill Robert	Prince George Co	100
Carling Joseph	Norfolk Co	200
Carling Walton	" "	50
Carnell Thomas	Nansemond Co	320
Carney John	Norfolk Co	100
Carney Richard	" "	100
Carpenter Charles	Northampton Co	240
Carr Robert	Nansemond Co	200
Carr Thomas	King William Co	500
Carraway John	Princess Anne Co	180
Carriell Tho.	Surry Co	100
Carter Coll	Middlesex Co	1150
Carter John on Fox's Island	Accomack Co	203
Carter Robert	Petso-Gloucester Co	1102
Carter Theod	Henrico Co	75
Carter Thom	Isle of Wight Co	700
Carter Timo	King & Queen Co	350
Carter -------	" "	300
Carter Wm.	Middlesex Co	170
Cartwright Jno	Princess Anne Co	100
Cartwright Peter	Norfolk Co	1050

		Acres
Cartwright Robert	Princess Anne Co	260
Cartwright Widdo	Norfolk Co	800
Carvy Richard	Northampton Co	100
Cary Edward	Abbington-Gloucester Co	100
Cary James	" " "	50
Cary Mr. Henry	Warwick Co	670
Cary Hugh	Essex Co	50
Cary Capt. Miles	Warwick Co	600
Cary Coll. Miles	" "	1960
Cary Maj. Wm.	" "	300
Case Hugh	New Kent Co	100
Casey Nicholas	Isle of Wight Co	550
Cason Thomas	Princess Anne Co	550
Caswell Widdo	Norfolk Co	350
Catherill Wm.	Princess Co	150
Cathern John	King William Co	180
Catlett John	Essex Co	1800
Catte Robert	Prince George Co	100
Caughlane James	King & Queen Co	100
Causebee James	York Co	200
Cawley Abraham	Warwick Co	80
Cawley Edward	York Co	150
Cearley Wm.	James City Co	450
Celar John	King William Co	100
Center John	James City Co	100
Chadwick Wm.	King William Co	150
Chamberlain Leon	Essex Co	350
Chamberlain Maj. Tho	Henrico Co	1000
Chambers Edward	New Kent Co	235
Chambers George	" " "	100
Chambers William	Surry Co	50
Chammins Henry	Prince George Co	300
Champion Edward	Isle of Wight Co	600
Champison Charles	Accomack Co	270
Chance Henry	" "	445
Chance William	" "	450
Chandler ffrancis	New Kent Co	150
Chandler John	Elizabeth City Co	150
Chandler Robert	New Kent Co	160
Chandler William	" " "	300
Chaney Widdo	Middlesex Co	800
Chapell James	Warwick Co	100
Chapell Robert	" "	150
Chapell Widdo	" "	321
Chapman Benjamin	Surry Co	500
Chapman Henry	Princess Anne Co	250
Chapman John	York Co	70
Chapman John	King & Queen Co	200
Chapman Mary	" " " "	200
Chapman Richard	Norfolk Co	50
Charles John	Accomack Co	480
Charles Phill	James City Co	200
Charles Capt. Thomas	Warwick Co	100
Charleton John	Norfolk Co	50
Charwill Robert	Elizabeth City Co	440
Chase Anne	Accomack Co	220

		Acres
Chawell Peter	Accomack Co	250
Cheatham Tho	Henrico Co	300
Checett James	Surry Co	50
Cheedle John	Middlesex Co	50
Cheesman Thom	Ware-Gloucester Co	650
Cheesman Thom senr	York Co	1800
Cheesman Thom junr	" "	600
Chekmore Edward	Norfolk Co	800
Cheney John	Essex Co	200
Cheney William	" "	700
Chesley Wm	New Kent Co	500
Chessum Alexandr	King & Queen Co	150
Chew Larkin	Essex Co	300
Chew Larkin	" "	550
Chichester Wm	Princess Anne Co	400
Chick Tho.	Northampton Co	100
Chilcott John	Nansemond Co	100
Childers Abr. senr	Henrico Co	368
Childers Abr. junr	" "	100
Childers Philip senr	" "	50
Childers Philip	" "	300
Childers Thomas	" "	300
Chiles Henry	King William Co	700
Chiles Henry	New Kent Co	700
Chilton Peter	Middlesex Co	100
Chin Hugh	King & Queen Co	100
Christian Thom	Charles City Co	1273
Church Richard (given Curch)	Norfolk Co	1050
Church Samuell	Northampton Co	143
Churchill Wm.	Middlesex Co	1950
Churey John	Norfolk Co	150
Churey Thomas	" "	100
Churey Widdow	" "	600
Claibourne John	King William Co	50
Claibourne Capt Tho	" "	1000
Claiborne Coll. Wm.	" " "	3000
Clark Daniell	Charles City Co	250
Clark Edward	" " "	962
Clark Edwd.	Middlesex Co	300
Clark James	Ware-Gloucester Co	250
Clark John	Henrico Co	300
Clarke John	Isle of Wight Co	850
Clarke John	Nansemond Co	25
Clark Jno	Surry Co	100
Clark Joseph	Accomack Co	200
Clark Joseph	Charles City Co	230
Clark Margaret	King William Co	100
Clark Robert	Surry Co	400
Clark Robert	Isle of Wight Co	450
Clark Thomas	Accomack Co	100
Clark William	Isle of Wight Co	600
Clark William	Henrico Co	333
Clarkson David	New Kent Co	200
Claunton Richard	Prince George Co	100
Claunton William	" " "	100
Clay John	" " "	350

		Acres
Clay Thom	Prince George Co	70
Clayton Jeremy	King & Queen Co	325
Clayton John	" " " "	400
Cleyton Susannah, widdow	" " " "	700
Cleake John	Petso-Gloucester Co	100
Cleaver Thom	Abbington-Gloucester Co	200
Cleg John senr	Northampton Co	204
Cleg Henry	" "	204
Clement Barthol. of England	Surry Co, one tract, tax due	
Clements Benjamin	Abbington-Gloucester Co	500
Clements Benjamin	" tax due King Wm.	600
Clements Benjamin	Petso-Gloucester Co	400
Clements Capt.	Prince George Co	1920
Clements ffrancis	Surry Co	600
Cleaments Jno	" "	387
Clent Grustam	Abbington-Gloucester Co	100
Clerk Alonson	Henrico Co	604
Clerk Christo	New Kent Co	300
Clerk Edwd	" " "	282
Clerk George	Northampton Co	833
Clerk Henry	York Co	100
Clerk John	Prince George Co	83
Clerk John	Northampton Co	100
Clerk Robert	James City Co	300
Clerk Sarah	" " "	200
Clerk Wm	" " "	1100
Clerk & Cordell of Gloucester	own King & Queen, tax pd.	1000
Clopton William	New Kent Co	454
Clough Capt.	" " "	80
Clough George	King and Queen Co	390
Coakes Robert	King William	100
Coates Samll	Essex Co	300
Coates William	King William Co	50
Coape Wm.	Northampton Co	200
Cob Samuell	" "	130
Cobb Edward	Nansemond Co	100
Cobb Ingold	Accomack Co	150
Cobb Mary	Isle of Wight Co	150
Cobb Robert	York Co	100
Cobbs Ambrose	James City Co	350
Cobbs Ambrose	York Co	163
Cobbs William	" "	50
Cobnall Symon	Essex Co	100
Cobson John	Petso-Gloucester Co	100
Cock Edward	Charles City Co	350
Cock Jonathon	James City Co	250
Cock Walter	Surry Co	875
Cock William	" "	630
Cocke James	Henrico Co	1506
Cocke James	Prince George Co	750
Cocke John	Henrico Co	98
Cocke Richard	" "	476
Cocke Richard, senr	" "	2180
Cocke Richard	Charles City Co	975
Cock Stephen for Jones' orphans	Prince George Co	2405
Cocke Capt. Thomas	Henrico Co	2976

Acres

Cocke Capt. Thomas	Princess Anne Co	800
Cocke William	Henrico Co	1535
Cocker John	Surry Co	900
Cocker William	New Kent Co	1000
Cockin Thom.	Essex Co	120
Cockin Wm.	Surry Co	100
Cockram Joseph	King William Co	600
Cockram William	" "	200
Codell Richard	Charles City Co	100
Coe Sarah	Accomack Co	900
Coe Timothy non resident	" " tax due	4100
Coefield Ann	Nansemond Co	300
Coefield Cresham	" "	350
Coefield Ruth	" "	110
Coignan Jacob	James City Co (with J. Danzee)	111
Cogwell Frederick	Essex Co	250
Cole's Coll. orphans	Warwick Co	1350
Cole John	Nansemond Co	814
Cole Richard	James City Co	80
Cole Robert	Charles City Co	80
Cole Robert	Accomack Co	125
Cole Sillvanus	" "	250
Cole William	" "	375
Cole William	Essex Co	200
Coleman Daniel	King & Queen Co	470
Coleman Francis	Prince George Co	150
Coleman George	" " "	200
Coleman John	Petso-Gloucester Co	200
Coleman Joseph	Abbington-Gloucester Co	200
Coleman Robert	Nansemond Co	1400
Coleman Robert	Isle of Wight Co	1500
Coleman Robert	Essex Co	450
Coleman Thomas	Abbington-Gloucester Co	250
Coleman Thomas	King & Queen Co	300
Coleman Wm. junr	Prince George Co	100
Collett Thomas	New Kent Co	100
Colley John	Norfolk Co	100
Collier Bartholomew	Northampton Co	150
Collier Charles	York Co	684
Collier Charles	King & Queen Co	450
Collier Gills	Princess Anne Co	500
Collier John	King & Queen Co	400
Collier John	Surry Co	3502
Collier Joseph	" "	40
Collier Mary	York Co	433
Collier Robert	King & Queen Co	100
Collier Thomas	Surry Co	550
Collings James	Nansemond Co	300
Collins James	King & Queen Co	300
Collins John	Accomack Co (with Asban)	1666
Collins John	" "	100
Collins William	Nansemond Co	1220
Collins William	King & Queen Co	350
Collins William	Norfolk Co	100
Collis Thomas	Ware-Gloucester Co	100
Collone Owen	Accomack Co	500

		Acres
Collone William	Petso-Gloucester Co	400
Colum Richard	New Kent Co	130
Coman William	York Co	50
Commins Benjamin	Princess Anne Co	200
Compton William	Essex Co	50
Condute Nathaniell	" "	20
Conner Lewis	Norfolk Co	2200
Conner Timothy	King & Queen Co	1410
Connis John	Princess Anne Co	175
Connoly Edward	Essex Co	200
Consalvins William	Accomack Co	100
Cook Abraham	New Kent Co	200
Cook Benjamin	King & Queen Co	200
Cook Capt.	Ware-Gloucester Co	1500
Cook Elizabeth	Surry Co	200
Cook Giles	Ware-Gloucester Co	140
Cook Jno	King & Queen Co	50
Cook John	Essex Co	112
Cook Reuben	Isle of Wight Co	250
Cook Richard	James City Co	75
Cook Thomas	Isle of Wight Co	300
Cook Thomas	Petso-Gloucester Co	350
Cook Thomas senr	King & Queen Co	100
Cook Thomas junr	" " "	50
Cook William	Warwick Co	29
Cook William	Petso-Gloucester Co	135
Cooley Charles	Elizabeth City Co	200
Cooper Cha:	" " "	100
Cooper Edward	Princess Anne Co	200
Cooper George senr	Elizabeth City Co	100
Cooper James	Surry Co	100
Cooper John	Norfolk Co	150
Cooper Joseph	Warwick Co	200
Cooper Joseph	Nansemond Co	267
Cooper Philip	Ware-Gloucester Co	200
Cooper Richard	Essex Co	100
Cooper Samuel	York Co	150
Cooper Thos	James City Co	60
Cooper Thos	Essex Co	100
Cooper William	" "	50
Cooper William	Norfolk Co	150
Copeland Christo	Elizabeth City Co	340
Copeland Francis	Nansemond Co	513
Copeland Henry	" "	150
Copeland James	" "	300
Copeland John	" "	600
Copland Jno	Essex Co	175
Copland Nicho	" "	300
Coper Thos	Accomack Co	711
Corbell Thomas	Nansemond Co	200
Corbin Coll.	Middlesex Co	2200
Corbin Gawin	Essex Co	2000
Corbin George	Northampton Co	250
Corbin George owns	Accomack Co	150
Corbin Gowin	King & Queen Co	2000
Corbin John	Nansemond Co	300

		Acres
Corbin Thomas	Essex Co	440
Corbin Thomas	Essex Co	4000
Cordell & Clerk of Gloucester . . .	own in King & Queen Co	1000
Corden Thomas	Norfolk Co	390
Cordey Thomas	New Kent.Co	150
Core Henry	Nansemond Co	50
Cormeck Mich	Northampton Co	100
Corneck Mr. Wm	Princess Anne Co	1974
Corprew John	Norfolk Co	650
Corprew Thom	" "	650
Cosby Charles	James City Co	250
Coslin John	Accomack Co	50
Costin ffrancis	Northampton Co	275
Cottell Thomas	Norfolk Co	200
Cotrell Richard	New Kent Co	200
Cotton Catherine	King & Queen Co	50
Cotton James	Warwick Co	70
Cotton John	Elizabeth City Co	50
Cotton John	Isle of Wight Co	200
Cotten Thomas	Surry Co	257
Cotten Walter	" "	257
Cotten William	Warwick Co	143
Couch Robert	Ware-Gloucester Co	100
Council Hardy	Isle of Wight Co	900
Council Hodges	" " "	420
Council John	" " "	760
County Land The	Warwick Co	150
Couzins Charles	Henrico Co	362
Covengton Richard	Essex Co	1000
Covington William	" "	400
Cowdry Josiah	Northampton Co	167
Cowles Thomas	James City Co	675
Cowling John	Nansemond Co	100
Cowling Michael	" "	100
Cox Bartholmew	Henrico Co	100
Cox John	" "	150
Cox John	York Co	50
Cox John	Northampton Co	500
Cox George	Henrico Co	200
Cox Richard	" "	300
Cox Richard	Princess Anne Co	50
Cox William	Essex Co	500
Cox William	Henrico Co	300
Cox William	New Kent Co	350
Cradock Samuell	King William Co	600
Crafort Carter	Surry Co	100
Crafort Robert	" "	1000
Cramore George	Norfolk Co	100
Crane Thomas	King & Queen Co	320
Crane William	" " "	120
Crane William	" " "	300
Cranke Nathaniel	Middlesex Co	50
Cranks Thomas	" "	54
Cranshaw Thomas	King William Co	150
Crawford David senr	New Kent Co	300
Crawford David junr	" " "	400

		Acres
Crawford Capt. Wm	Princess Anne Co	2650
Crawley Nathaniell	York Co	384
Crawley Robert	" "	400
Crawley Robert	James City Co	460
Cray Thomas	Kingston-Gloucester Co	200
Credle William	" " "	50
Creech Richard	Nansemond Co	200
Crekmore Edmund	Norfolk Co	690
Crekmore John	" "	750
Cretendon Richard	Ware-Gloucester Co	280
Crew John	Northampton Co	300
Crew Samuell orphans	Warwick Co	150
Crippen Thomas	Accomack Co	648
Crips Thomas	York Co	750
Crisp Tobias	King & Queen Co	100
Croashell Widow	Elizabeth City Co	100
Crockson land formerly, present owner ? tax due Pr. George		750
Crofton Francis	Accomack Co	200
Croley John	Warwick Co	100
Croucher orphans	" "	50
Crook George	Prince George Co	489
Crooker George	" " "	30
Croome Joell	New Kent Co	600
Croper Sebastian	Accomack Co	600
Crosby Peter	Princess Anne Co	250
Crow John	Essex Co	440
Crow Thomas	" "	300
Crowder Bartho	Prince George Co	75
Croxson Anne	Ware-Gloucester Co	300
Crozdall Roger	Henrico Co	200
Crump Elizabeth	New Kent Co	80
Crump James	" " "	150
Crump Richard	" " "	60
Crump Robert	" " "	150
Crump Stephen	" " "	60
Crump William	" " "	330
Crumpler Wm.	Isle of Wight Co	580
Crutchfield Peter	New Kent Co	400
Crutchfield Junr	" " "	400
Cryer George	James City Co	100
Crymes William	Petso-Gloucester Co	400
Cully Robert	Kingston-Gloucester Co	200
Curch (Church) Rich	Norfolk Co	1050
Curd Edward	Henrico Co	600
Curiton Thomas	Prince George Co	150
Curle Mr. Nicho	Elizabeth City Co	950
Curle Mr. Pasquo	" " "	300
Curnell Andrew	New Kent Co	30
Curtin Adam	Middlesex Co	200
Curtis Edward	York Co	200
Curtis James	Middlesex Co	300
Curtis Robert	York Co	250
Curtis Rose	Kingston-Gloucester Co	400
Custis Hancock	Northampton Co	50
Custis Henry	Accomack Co	774
Custis Coll. Jno. Esqr	" "	5950

24

		Acres
Custis Coll. Jno . . . . Northampton Co		3400
Custis Majr. Jno . . . . " "		3250
Custis William . . . . Accomack Co		1500
Cutchins Thomas . . . . Nansemond Co		150
Cuthrell Going . . . . Norfolk Co		470
Cutrell Thomas . . . . " "		150
Cutler Richard . . . . Accomack Co		450

------- D -------

		Acres
Dabney Benj . . . . King William Co		200
Dabney George . . . . " " "		290
Dabney James . . . . " " "		200
Dabony James . . . . New Kent Co		320
Daingerfield John . . . . Essex Co		270
Daingerfield Wm . . . . " "		270
Dalley Henry . . . . Norfolk Co		1524
Dalley William . . . . " "		156
Daniell Hugh . . . . " "		100
Daniell James . . . . Essex Co		100
Daniell James . . . . Middlesex Co		150
Daniell John . . . . New Kent Co		150
Daniell John . . . . York Co		200
Daniell Joseph . . . . Prince George Co		50
Daniell Richard . . . . Middlesex Co		210
Daniell Robert . . . . " "		225
Daniell Roger orphans . . . . Warwick Co		196
Daniell Thomas . . . . Prince George Co		150
Daniell William . . . . Accomack Co		200
Daniell Wm. . . . . Middlesex Co		150
Danzee Jno & J. Coignan . . . . . James City Co		4111
Darby Churchil . . . . Accomack Co		125
Darby William . . . . " "		83
Darden John . . . . Nansemond Co		500
Darnell Jerim . . . . Petso-Gloucester Co		150
Darnell John . . . . " " "		60
Darnell Rachell . . . . New Kent Co		100
Daughtie James . . . . Nansemond Co		400
Daughtree Lewis . . . . " "		100
Daughtree Wm . . . . " "		100
Daughty John . . . . Essex Co		200
Davenport Davis . . . . King William Co		200
Davenport Martin . . . . " " "		100
Davenport Mest . . . . New Kent Co		125
Davey ffrancis . . . . James City Co		778
David Thomas . . . . Essex Co		150
Davis Arthur . . . . Surry Co		460
Davis Arthur . . . . " "		50
Davis Christopher . . . . Prince George Co		50
Davis Christopher . . . . Elizabeth City Co		25
Davis Edwd . . . . King & Queen Co		100
Davis Edward . . . . Norfolk Co		300
Davis Edward . . . . Princess Anne Co		200
Davis Edward . . . . Warwick Co		200

Acres

Davis Eliazar	New Kent Co	375
Davis Evans	Essex Co	150
Davis Francis	Isle of Wight Co	100
Davis George	James City Co	50
Davis James	Accomack Co	1100
Davis John	Isle of Wight Co	250
Davis John . . . tax due one tract in Surry Co		
Davis John	King William Co	200
Davis John	Northampton Co	850
Davis John	New Kent Co	80
Davis John	Middlesex Co	100
Davis John	King & Queen Co	90
Davis Lewis	King William Co	200
Davis Moses	Elizabeth City Co	150
Davis Nathaniel	Surry Co	157
Davis Nathll	King & Queen Co	300
Davis Owen	York Co	247
Davis Richard	Charles City Co	118
Davis Robert	Accomack Co	384
Davis Robert	King William Co	200
Davis Thomas	Charles City Co	200
Davis Thomas	Isle of Wight Co	100
Davis Thomas	Norfolk Co	332
Davis Thomas	" "	340
Davis Thomas	Nansemond Co	340
Davis Thomas	" "	144
Davis Thomas	" "	250
Davis Widdo	Kingston-Gloucester Co	360
Davis William	Elizabeth City Co	42
Davis William	King William Co	200
Davis William senr	Norfolk Co	250
Davis William	" "	158
Davis William	Prince George Co	100
Davis William	York Co	200
Davis William	" "	100
Davison James	Ware-Gloucester Co	100
Davill Paltey	Elizabeth City Co	100
Davill Samuel	" " "	100
Dawes William	Isle of Wight Co	400
Dawson Henry	Warwick Co	200
Dawson John	" "	300
Dawson John	Ware-Gloucester Co	780
Dawson Samuel	" " "	350
Day Alexander	King & Queen Co	300
Day John	Petso-Gloucester Co	400
Day Richard	Essex Co	100
Dayley Owen	King & Queen Co	180
Deadman Phil	York Co	75
Deall Benj	Isle of Wight Co	467
Deane John	James City Co	150
Dean Richd	Surry Co	100
Deane Thomas	James City Co	80
Deane Thomas	" " "	150
Deane William	" " "	100
Dearemore Robert	Princess Anne Co	514
Deberry Peter	Isle of Wight Co	100

		Acres
Debnam Capt. Wm	Ware-Gloucester Co	1250
Delby Margery	Northampton Co	450
Dellistations Sebastian sr	Accomack Co	500
Dellistations Sebastian jr	" "	400
Delk Roger	Surry Co	790
Denbigh Psh. Gleab	Warwick Co	130
Denby Hector	Princess Anne Co	600
Denby Edward	Norfolk Co	100
Dennett John	New Kent Co	350
Dennis Timothy	Princess Anne Co	100
Denson John	Isle of Wight Co	200
Dent Tho. non-resident	Accomack Co tax due	500
Denton Thomas	Northampton Co	400
Deprest Robert	New Kent Co	350
Derby Daniell sr	Accomack Co	300
Derby Daniell jr	" "	125
Derby Dorman	" "	225
Deshazo Peter	King & Queen Co	450
Devillard Jacob	Essex Co	80
Dewis Richard	King & Queen Co	250
Dewy George	Northampton Co	300
Dewy Jacob	" "	100
Dibdall John	New Kent Co	800
Dickason Thomas	King William Co	100
Dickason William	" " "	100
Dicks James	Surry Co	400
Dicks Thomas	Essex Co	500
Dickson William	Accomack Co (for Littleton)	1050
Didlake James	King & Queen Co	200
Diggs Dudley	York Co	1350
Diggs Coll. Dudley	Warwick Co	4626
Diggs Coll. Dudley	Elizabeth City Co	216
Diggs John	Kingston-Gloucester Co	1200
Dilliard Edward	King & Queen Co	150
Dillard George	" " "	325
Dilliard Nicho	" " "	150
Dillard Thomas	" " "	170
Dillon Henry	King William Co	150
Dimmock Thomas	King & Queen Co	150
Dismukes William	" " "	200
Dison Nicholas	Henrico Co	150
Dix Isaac	Accomack Co	500
Dix John	" "	500
Dixon Christopher	Kingston-Gloucester Co	300
Dixon John	Norfolk Co	300
Dixon Michaell	Northampton Co	460
Dixon Nicho	Nansemond Co	200
Dixon Richard	York Co	450
Dixon Richard	Abbington-Gloucester	200
Dixon Thomas	Petso-Gloucester Co	300
Doage Mr James	Princess Anne Co	784
Dobbins Daniell	Essex Co	550
Dobson Edmund	Abbington-Gloucester Co	350
Dobson John	" " "	400
Dobson ffrancis	Middlesex Co	150
Dobson William	Abbington-Gloucester Co	950

		Acres
Doby John	James City Co	300
Doby John	Prince George Co	500
Docton Thomas	Nansemond Co	200
Dodd John	New Kent Co	300
Dodson William	Henrico Co	100
Doe William	King & Queen Co	300
Dolerd Wm	New Kent Co	50
Doley John	Princess Anne Co	640
Doller Joseph	" " "	150
Donas Arthur	Accomack Co	100
Doonall William	Norfolk Co	100
Dormar John	James City Co	100
Dorrell Sampson	Ware-Gloucester Co	300
Dorrell Sampson	King William Co	5000
Doswell John	York Co	367
Doswell John jr	" "	100
Douglas Charles	Henrico Co	63
Douglas William	King William Co	200
Dowie John	Middlesex Co	75
Dowing George	Prince George Co	100
Dowles John	Isle of Wight Co	150
Dowman John	Northampton Co	100
Downer John	King William Co	300
Downes Elias	" " "	300
Downing John	Northampton Co	70
Dowty Rowland	" "	150
Doyley Cope	Warwick Co	500
Draught Richard	Princess Anne Co	500
Drawler Abr	Isle of Wight Co	200
Drayton Roger	Prince George Co	270
Dresdall Robert	Norfolk Co	318
Dressall Timo	Essex Co	175
Drew Edward	Surry Co	600
Drew Thomas	" "	800
Drewett John	York Co	200
Druer John	Isle of Wight Co	100
Drument John	Petso-Gloucester Co	80
Drummond Hill	Accomack Co	483
Drummond John	James City Co	700
Drummond John	Accomack Co	1550
Drummond Richard	" "	600
Drummond Stephen	" "	300
Drummond William	James City Co	150
Drury Capt. Chas	Nansemond Co	570
Drury John	" "	87
Drury Thomas	" "	75
Drury William	" "	80
Duberry Samuel	Warwick Co	200
Duck William	Isle of Wight Co	180
Duckitt Abraham	James City Co	290
Dudding Andrew	Essex Co	230
Dudley Ambrose	Kingston-Gloucester Co	?
Dudley Capt.	" " "	650
Dudley Christo	Nansemond Co	200
Dudley James	Middlesex Co	200
Dudley James	Petso-Gloucester Co	780

		Acres
Dudley Richard	Petso-Gloucester Co	400
Dudley Richard	Kingston-Gloucester Co	350
Dudley Richard	Ware-Gloucester Co	300
Dudley Robert	Middlesex Co	300
Dudley Thomas	" "	200
Dudley Thomas	Petso-Gloucester Co	200
Duelt Charles	King & Queen Co	900
Duffield William	Nansemond Co	50
Duglas James	King & Queen Co	275
Duglas John	Prince George Co	300
Duke Henry Esq	New Kent Co	325
Duke Henry Esq	" " "	170
Duke Henry Esq	James City Co	2986
Duke Henry junr	" " "	1000
Duke Henry	York Co	25
Duke John	Nansemond Co	113
Duke Thomas	" "	400
Duke Thomas junr	" "	930
Duke Thomas	James City Co	750
Dullard Henry	Isle of Wight Co	100
Dullock John	Northampton Co	100
Dumas Jeremiah	New Kent Co	250
Duncon David	Princess Anne Co	100
Dunkin Thomas	Prince George Co	136
Dunkley John	King & Queen Co	380
Dunn Henry	Elizabeth City Co	50
Dunn Mrs or Mr. Merry	" " "	500
Dunn William	" " "	100
Dunn William	Essex Co	220
Dunton Benjamin	Northampton Co	220
Dunton John	" "	170
Dunton Joseph	" "	120
Dunton Thomas senr	" "	400
Dunton Thomas junr	" "	120
Dunton William	" "	420
Duparks Thomas	" "	90
Dupra Giles	Elizabeth City Co	150
Durden Jacob	Isle of Wight Co	500
Durding Richard	Prince George Co	500
Durham James	New Kent Co	100
Durham John	King & Queen Co	100
Durrat Widdo	" " "	200
Duson Thomas	" " "	448
Dyatt Thomas	Middlesex Co	200
Dyer Henry	York Co	50
Dyer Jeffrey	Essex Co	100
Dyer John	Accomack Co	200
Dyer William	Princess Anne Co	700
Dyer William	Essex Co	100

------- E -------

		Acres
Eachols John	King & Queen Co	220
Ealam Martin	Henrico Co	130
Ealam Robert	" "	400
Ease Peter	Accomack Co	250
Eason John	Nansemond Co	150
Eason Peter	" "	400
Eason William	" "	180
East Edward	Henrico Co	150
East Thomas senr	" "	475
East Thomas	" "	554
Easter Grace	Ware-Gloucester Co	200
Easter John	" " "	350
Eastes Abraham	King & Queen Co	200
Eastham Edward	" " "	100
Eastham Edward junr	" " "	800
Eastham George	" " "	300
Eaton John	York Co	170
Edmonds John	Norfolk Co	50
Edmonds Thomas	York Co	150
Edmondson James	Essex Co	500
Edmondson Thomas	" "	700
Edmunds David	Northampton Co	500
Edmunds Elizabeth	James City Co	175
Edmund Howell	Surry Co	300
Edmunds Jeremiah	Nansemond Co	70
Edmund William	Surry Co	100
Edwards Abraham	Nansemond	400
Edwards Charles	Isle of Wight Co	400
Edwards Elizabeth	Princess Anne Co	50
Edward James	King William Co	353
Edwards John	King & Queen Co	100
Edwards John	Kingston-Gloucester Co	534
Edwards John	Charles City Co	287
Edwards John	Norfolk Co	250
Edwards John	Surry Co	470
Edwards Nathaniell	Warwick Co	100
Edwards Robert	Isle of Wight Co	150
Edwards Thomas	Henrico Co	676
Edwards Thomas	Prince George Co	250
Edward Mr. William	Surry Co	2755
Edwards William	Nansemond Co	150
Eglestone Benjamin	James City Co	1375
Eggleston Joseph	" " "	550
Egny Elizabeth	King William Co	100
Elderkin John	New Kent Co	300
Ele Samuell	Charles City Co	682
Elerby Elizabeth	James City Co	600
Elkes John	Princess Anne Co	500
Elkes Robert	Nansemond Co	175
Elkes William	" "	100
Elliott Alice	Essex Co	75
Elliott Anthony	Ware-Gloucester Co	100
Elliott James	King William Co	1700

		Acres
Elliott Robert	Kingston-Gloucester Co	1247
Elliott William	" " "	1060
Elliott Thomas	King William Co	480
Ellis Edward	Surry Co	30
Ellis James	" "	170
Ellis James	" "	180
Ellis Jere	" "	50
Ellis John senr	Prince George Co	400
Ellis John junr	" " "	400
Ellis John	Henrico Co	217
Ellis John	King & Queen Co	400
Ellis Joseph	Nansemond Co	290
Ellis Robert	Prince George Co	50
Ellis Timothy	King & Queen Co	350
Ellis William	New Kent Co	100
Ellis William	Norfolk Co	200
Ellison Garratt Robt	Surry Co	520
Ellitt William	" "	250
Elly Richard	King William Co	100
Elmore Peter	New Kent Co	100
Elmore Thomas	" "	300
Elmore Thomas jr	" " "	100
Emperor Mr. Francis	Princess Anne Co	400
Emperor Tully	" " "	300
Emory Ralph	King & Queen Co	100
England William	New Kent Co	490
English Mungo	" " "	500
English Thomas	Isle of Wight Co	100
Entroughty Derby	Henrico Co	200
Epes Dan	Prince George Co	200
Epes Edward	" " "	500
Epes Capt. Francis	" " "	226
Epes Capt. Francis	Henrico Co	2145
Epes Francis jr	" "	444
Epes Isham	" "	444
Epes John sen	Prince George Co	530
Epes John	" " "	300
Epes John	Charles City Co	500
Epes Littlebury	" " "	400
Epes Littlebury	Prince George Co	833
Epes William sr	" " "	750
Epes William	" " "	633
Eperson John	New Kent Co	120
Esdoll Edward	Northampton Co	100
Esdoll George	" "	100
Eshon John	" "	600
Estwood John	Norfolk Co	75
Estwood Thomas	" "	170
Etherdge Charles	" "	75
Etherdge Marmeduke	" "	525
Etherdge Edwd. Cooper	" "	200
Etherdge Edwd. senr	" "	33
Etherdge Edward	" "	66
Etherdge Tho. Cooper	" "	75
Etherdge Thomas B.R.	" "	50
Etherdge Thomas senr	" "	34

		Acres
Etherdge Thomas junr	Norfolk Co	33
Ethredge William	" "	250
Ethredge Wm. junr	" "	80
Etherington Thomas	Princess Anne Co	108
Evans Abraham	Surry Co	150
Evans Abrigall	Norfolk Co	100
Evans Anthony	Surry Co	100
Evans Benjamin	Prince George Co	700
Evans Charles	Henrico Co	225
Evans John	Accomack Co	200
Evans John	Charles City Co	800
Evans John	Northampton Co	200
Evans John	Prince George Co	800
Evans Mary	" " "	400
Evans Peter	" " "	270
Evans Rice	Essex Co	200
Evans Sarah	Accomack Co	150
Evans Thomas	Northampton Co	300
Evell Charles	Accomack Co	550
Evell Marke	" "	250
Evell Solomon	" "	125
Everett Simon	Isle of Wight Co	1100
Everett William	Nansemond Co	150
Evitt Thomas	Essex Co	100
Ewbank William	King & William Co	350
Exam Francis	Isle of Wight Co	200
Exam Jeremiah	" " " "	300
Exam William	" " " "	1440
Exam William	" " " "	150
Exum Sarah	Nansemond Co	150
Eyes Cornelius	King & Queen Co	100
Eyres Anne, widdo	Northampton Co	733
Eyres Capt. John	" "	744
Eyres Nicholas	" "	325
Eyres Thomas	" "	1133
Ezell George	Surry Co	150

------- F -------

Fabin Paul	Northampton Co	60
Faile John	Henrico Co	240
Failton Roger	Isle of Wight Co	237
Fairfax James	Accomack Co	900
Falliham Morriss orphans	Prince George Co. & Rob River	200
Farguson James	King & Queen Co	300
Farish Robert	" " " "	1400
Farloe John senr	Henrico Co	100
Farloe John junr	" "	551
Farmer Henry	" "	100
Farmer John	King & Queen Co tax due	250
Farmer Samuell	Nansemond Co	160
Farrar John	Henrico Co	600
Farrar Thomas	" "	1444

		Acres
Farrar Capt. Wm.	Henrico Co	700
Farrell Charles	Essex Co	50
Farthing William	James City Co	50
Faulkner Edward	Essex Co	530
Faulkner Nicholas	" "	100
Faulkner Thomas	Elizabeth City Co	50
Fear Thomas	York Co	100
Fear Thomas junr	York Co	130
Feare Edmund	New Kent Co	200
Fearecloth Thomas	James City Co	277
Fellows Robert	Prince George Co	418
Fenton Widdo	New Kent Co	270
Ferbey John	Norfolk Co	500
Ferguson John	Essex Co	150
Ferguson Robert	Henrico Co	230
Fergison Thomas	Norfolk Co	100
Ferisby Benjamin	Surry Co	170
Ferris Richard senr	Henrico Co	550
Ferriss William	" "	50
Fetherstone Henry	" "	700
ffield John.	Prince George Co	100
Field Major Peter	Henrico Co	2185
Fielding Henry	King & Queen Co	1000
Finch Edward	New Kent Co	300
Finey William	Accomack Co	800
ffingall Samuell.	Elizabeth City Co	333
Finley William	Middlesex Co	50
Finton Frances	King William Co	100
Fips John.	York Co	150
Fish John	James City Co	100
Fisher Benjamin	Essex Co	150
Fisher Jonotham	" "	250
Fisher John.	Northampton Co	637
Fisher John, Accomack tax due on	" "	200
Fisher John.	Accomack Co	200
Fisher Phillip	" "	433
Fisher Thomas	Northampton Co	637
Fisher Thomas	Tax due Accomack Co	133
ffisher William	New Kent Co	100
Fitchott Joshua.	Northampton Co	100
Fitchott Joshua	Accomack Co	200
Fithgerreld Henry	Princess Anne Co	200
Flake Robert	Surry Co	200
Flanders Francis	James City Co	350
Fleming Charles	King William Co	1700
ffleming Charles	New Kent Co	920
Flemin Lawrence	Surry Co	360
Fleming William	Petso-Gloucester Co	600
Fletcher William	Accomack Co	200
Fliping Thomas	Kingston-Gloucester Co	300
Flipp John	King & Queen Co	80
Flood Elizabeth.	Prince George Co	100
Flood Thomas.	Surry Co	150
Flood Walter	Surry Co	820
Flowers Isaac.	Essex Co	250
Flowers Richard	Accomack Co	200

Acres

		Acres
Frame Arthur	Accomack Co	500
Francis John.	Elizabeth City Co	25
Francis Robert	Ware-Gloucester Co	400
Francis Robert	Abbington-Gloucester Co	104
Francis Thomas	New Kent Co	150
Francisco Dan	Northampton Co	150
Frank John	" "	500
Frank Thomas	Essex Co	175
Franklin James senr	Henrico Co	250
Franklin James junr	" " tax due on 360	786
Franklin Nicholas	Essex Co	130
Franklin Symon	Princess Anne Co	100
Frayser John	James City Co	250
Freeman George	" " "	197
ffreeman Henry	Middlesex Co	200
Freeman John	Norfolk Co	190
Freeman John	Prince George Co	300
Freeman Robert	Ware-Gloucester Co	135
Freeman William	New Kent Co	200
Freshwater George	Northampton Co	200
Freshwater William	" "	200
Frith Joseph	York Co	50
Frizell George	Northampton Co	140
Frost Thomas	" "	100
Frost William	Prince George Co	50
Fullalove Thomas	King William Co	100
Fuller Anthony	King William Co	150
Fuller Edward	York Co	70
Fullerton James	Essex Co	400
Fulsken John	Norfolk Co	1396
Furrbush Wm	James City Co	400
Furgison Tho.	Norfolk Co	100

------- G -------

Gabriell Richard	Middlesex Co	30
Gadberry Edward	King & Queen Co	100
Gadberry Thomas	New Kent Co	200
Gaines Barnerd	Essex Co	450
Gaithwaite Ephriam	Henrico Co	163
Gaithwaite Samuell.	" "	50
Gaitwood John	Essex Co	400
Gale Matthew junr	Kingston-Gloucester Co	250
Gamble Major Thomas	King & Queen Co	450
Games John	Essex Co	475
Gannock William	" "	2100
Garcond John	Isle of Wight Co	100
Gardner Elizabeth	" " " "	100
Gardner John	" " " "	246
Gardner Ringing	King & Queen Co	200
Gardner William	Middlesex Co	100
Garen Daniell	Norfolk Co	50
Garey Thomas	James City Co	60
Garland Edward	New Kent Co	2600

		Acres
Garland John	Isle of Wight Co	100
Garman William	Accomack Co	475
Garnet John	Kingston-Gloucester Co	250
Garnett John	Essex Co	150
Garrat James	New Kent Co	375
Garratt Thomas	King William Co	200
Garrett Daniell	King & Queen Co	200
Garrett Humphrey	" " " "	200
Garrett John	" " " "	330
Garrett Robert	" " " "	200
Garrett Thomas	Essex Co	1000
Garrison Richard	Accomack Co	468
Garves Jeffry	Abbington-Gloucester Co	33
Garwood Thomas	Kingston-Gloucester Co	77
Gascoyne Robert	Northampton Co	125
Gascoyne William	" "	525
Gatlin John	Nansemond Co	200
Gatlin William	" "	100
Gawdin William	Essex Co	100
Gawin Christo junr	Nansemond Co	20
Gawen Phillip	New Kent Co	50
Gay John	Nansemond Co	200
Gayle Capt.	Kingston-Gloucester Co	164
Gayle Thomas	Isle of Wight Co	200
Gebb Mr Thomas	Elizabeth City Co	630
Geddes ?	James City Co	476
Gee Charles	Prince George Co	484
Gee Henry	Henrico Co tax due on 10a	435
Geeres Thomas	King William Co	100
Gentry Nicho	New Kent Co	250
George David	Middlesex Co	150
George John	Isle of Wight Co	200
George Richard	King & Queen Co	100
George Robert	Middlesex Co	180
Gibbins Henry	Accomack Co	250
Gibbins Thomas	York Co	100
Gibbs Capt. John	Princess Anne Co	3100
Gibbs Henry	Warwick Co	315
Gibbs William	York Co	50
Gibons John	York Co	50
Gibson Gibey	James City Co	150
Gibson Hubert	Prince George Co	250
Gibson Jonothan	Essex Co	700
Gibson Thom.	New Kent Co	370
Gibson Widdo	King & Queen Co	200
Giddens Thom.	Northampton Co	227
Gilby John	King & Queen Co	300
Giles John	New Kent Co	120
Giles John	Isle of Wight Co	1150
Giles Thom	" " " "	880
Gilford Richard	York Co	100
Gill John	James City Co	100
Gill John	Henrico Co	235
Gill Nicho	New Kent Co	222
Gill Robert	Northampton Co	200
Gillam Charles	Prince George Co	200

		Acres
Gillam John	Prince George Co	1000
Gilley Grewin Arrian	Henrico Co	2528
Gillham Hincha	Surry Co	658
Gilligan Fernando	Norfolk Co	182
Gilligan John	" "	200
Gillmott John	New Kent Co	160
Gillmott Richard	" " "	150
Gills John	" " "	100
Ginings Phill.	James City Co	400
Glading John	Accomack Co	207
Gland Catherine	" "	217
Glanvills Richd orphans	Warwick Co	165
Glascock Richd	Kingston-Gloucester Co	500
Glass Anne	New Kent Co	150
Glass Thomas	" " "	150
Glassbrook Robert	" " "	400
Gleam John	" " "	300
Glover John	Essex Co	100
Glover William	King William Co	100
Glyn Widdo	Isle of Wight Co	390
Gobbee Edward	Middlesex Co	90
Godfrey John	Princess Anne Co	170
Godfrey Matt	" " "	150
Godfry John	Norfolk Co	1470
Godfry Matthew	" "	450
Godfry Waren	" "	350
Godwin Coll.	Isle of Wight Co	600
Godwin Devorix	Northampton Co	600
Godwin Capt Edwin	Nansemond Co	800
Godwin Coll Thom.	" "	810
Godwin Edmund	Isle of Wight Co	400
Godwin Joseph	" " " "	250
Godwin William	" " " "	400
Goelightly Hugh	Prince George Co	500
Goelightly John	" " "	100
Goffogan Thomas	Northampton Co	100
Gogni David	" "	150
Golden John	Warwick Co	50
Goldham Henry	Isle of Wight Co	1000
Good John senr	Henrico Co	600
Good John	King & Queen Co	200
Good Richard	Essex Co	200
Good Samuell	Henrico Co	588
Goodall John	James City Co	400
Goodgame David	Prince George Co	479
Goodger John	New Kent Co	200
Goodin Major quarter	King William Co	200
Goodloe George	Middlesex Co	50
Goodman John	James City Co	275
Goodman William	Surry Co	200
Goodrich Benjamin	James City Co	1650
Goodrich Charles	Isle of Wight Co	80
Goodrich John	Middlesex Co	50
Goodrich Major	Prince George Co	900
Goodring Alexander	New Kent Co	100
Goodson John	Ware-Gloucester Co	150

		Acres
Goodwin Elizabeth	York Co	1200
Goodwin Isaac	Warwick Co	225
Goodwin Peter	York Co	400
Goodwin Robert	James City Co	150
Goodwin Thomas	Prince George Co	150
Goodwin Capt. Thomas junr	Nansemond Co	697
Goodwin Ursula	" "	100
Gord Richard	Prince George Co	100
Gorden John	Nansemond Co	330
Gorden William	York Co	150
Gore Daniel	Accomack Co	3976
Gorton John	New Kent Co	250
Gosling William	" " "	460
Goss Charles	James City Co	171
Gough Alice widdo	King & Queen Co	800
Gough Hugh	Nansemond Co	150
Gough Richard	Warwick Co	60
Gough Thomas	Nansemond Co	150
Gould Price	Essex Co	200
Goulding Edward	Essex Co	380
Goulding John	Essex Co	200
Goulding William	Essex Co	200
Gouldman Francis	Essex Co	300
Gower James	Henrico Co - for Grigs land	500
Gowing Edward	Kingston-Gloucester Co	100
Grace Thomas	Isle of Wight Co	160
Grady Phillip	Abbington-Gloucester Co	150
Grady Phillip	Ware-Gloucester Co	200
Graham Thomas	New Kent Co	250
Granchaw Thomas	" " "	480
Grandberry Anne	Nansemond Co	75
Grandberry William	" "	300
Granger John	Henrico Co	472
Grant William	Princess Anne Co	150
Grathmee Owen	Abbington-Gloucester Co	250
Gravatt Henry	King William Co	150
Graves John	" " "	100
Graves John	King & Queen Co	150
Graves Joseph	James City Co	250
Graves Robert	King & Queen Co	150
Graves Thomas	Abbington-Gloucester Co	70
Gray Abner	Essex Co	350
Gray James	Accomack Co	900
Gray John	" "	116
Gray John	Surry Co	200
Gray Joseph	King & Queen Co	200
Gray Samuell	King & Queen Co	40
Gray Capt. William	Surry Co	1750
Gray Wm. jr	" "	1050
Gray Wm	" "	100
Green Darcas	Petso-Gloucester Co	400
Green Edward	New Kent Co	200
Green Edwd.	Surry Co	200
Green George	Isle of Wight Co	250
Green George	Essex Co	300
Greene John senr	Northampton Co	2200

		Acres
Green John	King William Co	100
Green John	Prince George Co	125
Green Lewis	" " "	149
Green Richd	Surry Co	260
Green Richard	Nansemond Co	200
Green Robert	York Co	200
Green Samuell	Essex Co	97
Green Sarah	Kingston-Gloucester Co	200
Green Thomas	James City Co	500
Green Thomas	" " "	50
Green William	" " "	100
Green Widdo	Kingston-Gloucester Co	150
Green William	Isle of Wight Co	150
Greenaway Christo	Ware-Gloucester Co	270
Greenfield ffrancis	New Kent Co	80
Grefen John	Norfolk Co	200
Gregory Anthony	Ware-Gloucester Co	700
Gregory Frances, widdo	King & Queen Co	700
Gregory Nicho	James City Co	50
Greithian James	Prince George Co	363
Gresham Edward	King & Queen Co	175
Gresham George	" " "	150
Gresham John	" " "	200
Gresham Thomas	" " "	225
Greswell Walter	Ware-Gloucester Co	50
Grice Aristotle	James City Co	700
Grice Peter	Northampton Co	200
Griffen Charles	Princess Anne Co	216
Griffen David	King & Queen Co	100
Griffen Edwd	" " "	100
Griffen James	Nansemond Co	500
Griffen James	Prince George Co	100
Griffen John	Surry Co	200
Griffen John	Accomack Co	150
Griffen Thomas	Essex Co	200
Griffin Thomas	Princess Anne Co	200
Griffith Benjamin	Northampton Co	200
Griffith Jeremiah	" "	345
Griffith Richard	Prince George Co	335
Grigg William	" " "	200
Griggs Antho.	Elizabeth City Co	50
Griggs ffrancis	King & Queen Co	250
Grigson Thomas	Essex Co	300
Grimes Capt.	Middlesex Co	900
Grimes James	Norfolk Co	150
Grimes John	" "	50
Grimmall Wm.	Essex Co	100
Grindall Richard	Accomack Co	350
Grindge Richard	New Kent Co	225
Grines Hustis	Surry Co	100
Grinley Susannah	Petso-Gloucester Co	200
Grinto William	Princess Anne Co	650
Groce Thomas	Isle of Wight Co	160
Grosse Edward	Charles City Co	100
Grout John	Petso-Gloucester Co	300
Groves Samuel	Warwick Co	490

Acres

Grundy William	Kingston-Gloucester Co	200
Grymes John	Petso-Gloucester Co	1400
Guest George	Middlesex Co	50
Guilsby Thomas	James City Co	300
Gullding Charles	Northampton Co	200
Gully Richard	Surry Co	50
Gumms Anthony	Nansemond Co	50
Gunn James	Charles City Co	250
Gunter Edward	Accomack Co	600
Gurrow William	York Co	150
Gutchins Joseph	Nansemond Co	250
Guttery John	King & Queen Co	230
Guy James (or Gvy)	Norfolk Co	100
Guy John	" "	110
Gwalney William	Surry Co	225
Gwalney William	" "	400
Gwin Capt.	Kingston-Gloucester Co	1100
Gwin Christo.	Nansemond Co	1010
Gwin David.	Essex Co	950
Gwin John	James City Co	100
Gwin William	Norfolk Co	350
Gwyn Rowland.	Nansemond Co	75

------- H -------

Hack Coll. Nicho Geo.	Accomack Co	2700
Hackley Henry	Nansemond Co	210
Hackney Widdo	Middlesex Co	300
Hadgeon Widdo	King & Queen Co	200
Hadley Ambrose	Isle of Wight Co	100
Hadley Dyonitia	James City Co	100
Haffield Capt. Luke	? tax due in Nansemond Co	
Hagard David Non-resident	Accomack Co	130
Hages Walter	" "	130
Haggaman Isaac	Northampton Co	750
Hail John	Essex Co	900
Hairy John	New Kent Co	280
Haiselwood John	" " "	200
Haiselwood Thomas	" " "	50
Haley James	James City Co	310
Hall Edward	Henrico Co	184
Hall ffrancis Widdo	Northampton Co	340
Hall Instance	Prince George Co	614
Hall Isaac	" " "	450
Hall John	James City Co	50
Hall John	Abbington-Gloucester Co	125
Hall Moses	Nansemond Co	95
Hall Poole	Isle of Wight Co	350
Hall Robert	Petso-Gloucester Co	100
Hall Robert	" " "	250
Hall Thomas	Princess Anne Co	400
Ham Richard	Surry Co	75
Hambleton James	Henrico Co	100
Hambleton John	Nansemond Co	200

		Acres
Hamlin Elizabeth	Prince George Co	250
Hamlin John	" " "	1484
Hamlin Mr. John.	non-res. tax due Surry Co	100
Hamlin John	Charles City Co	143
Hamlin Richard	Prince George Co	240
Hamlin Stephen	Charles City Co	80
Hamlin Thomas	" " "	264
Hamner Nicho	James City Co	500
Hampton John	King William Co	50
Hampton William	Kingston-Gloucester Co	348
Hanby Charles	Northampton Co	25
Hanby Daniell	" "	50
Hanby John	" "	150
Hanby Richard	" "	75
Hancock Colin	Surry Co	60
Hancock Robert	Henrico Co	860
Hancock Samuell	" "	100
Hancock Symon senr	Princess Anne Co	300
Hancock Symon junr	" " "	200
Hand Thomas	King & Queen Co	150
Handberry ?	Norfolk Co	300
Handcock Robert	James City Co	300
Handcock Thomas	King William Co	200
Handcock Thomas	Nansemond Co	30
Handiford John	Middlesex Co	100
Handley William	New Kent Co	150
Hanes John	Petso-Gloucester Co	150
Hanfield Michael	James City Co	50
Hankins Charles	New Kent Co	340
Hansell John	Warwick Co	100
Hansford Elizabeth	York Co	100
Hansford John	" "	100
Hansford Thomas.	Warwick Co	75
Hansford Thomas.	York Co	75
Hansford William	" "	300
Hansford William.	Petso-Gloucester Co	500
Harde Thomas	Surry Co	900
Hardgrove Wm	King & Queen Co	100
Hardiman John	Prince George Co	872
Hardy Richard	Isle of Wight Co	700
Hare Ann	Nansemond Co	600
Hare John.	" "	190
Hargrave Benj	Norfolk Co	250
Hargrove Bryan	Surry Co	100
Harlow Thom	New Kent Co	230
Harmon Elizabeth	Charles City Co	479
Harmon Henry	Essex Co	752
Harmon William	New Kent Co	350
Harmonson George	Northampton Co	1586
Harmonson Henry	" "	1250
Harmonson John	" "	1600
Harmonson Thom.	" "	400
Harmonson Capt Wm	" "	308
Harper John	Petso-Gloucester Co	100
Harper John	Essex Co	748
Harper Thomas.	" "	350

		Acres
Harper William	Essex Co	240
Harrald Thomas	Nansemond Co	652
Harrald Thomas	" "	100
Harrelston Paul	New Kent Co	360
Harris Benjamin	" " "	100
Harris Edmd	" " "	100
Harris Edward	Isle of Wight Co	240
Harris Edward	" " " "	100
Harris John	" " " "	365
Harris John	New Kent Co	146
Harris John	Nansemond Co	600
Harris John	Norfolk Co	110
Harris Joseph	Elizabeth City Co	50
Harris Mary	Henrico Co	94
Harris Robert	New Kent Co	75
Harris Thomas	" " "	100
Harris Thomas	Isle of Wight Co	350
Harris Thomas	Henrico Co	357
Harris Timothy	" "	250
Harris William	King & Queen Co	250
Harris William	James City Co	140
Harris William	Surry Co	150
Harris William	New Kent Co	150
Harris William	" " "	125
Harris William	" " "	100
Harrison Alex	Accomack Co	400
Harrison Andrew	Essex Co	300
Harrison Arnold	Accomack Co	630
Harrison Benj. Coll.	Surry Co	2750
Harrison Benj. jr.	James City Co	100
Harrison Benjamin	Charles City Co	6350
Harrison Coll. Esqr.	Prince George Co	150
Harrison Daniell	Surry Co	70
Harrison Gabriell	Prince George Co	150
Harrison Henry	Princess Anne Co	300
Harrison James	Essex Co	400
Harrison James	Prince George Co	300
Harrison Capt. Nath	Surry Co	2177
Harrison Robert	York Co	250
Harrison Robert	" "	200
Harrison Selby	Accomack Co	50
Harrison Capt Thom	non-res, tax due Surry Co	530
Harrison Thom	Prince George Co	1077
Harrison Wm.	" " "	1930
Harrison Wm.	James City Co	150
Harrison Wm.	York Co	50
Hart Henry	Surry Co	725
Hart Robert	" "	600
Hart Thomas	King & Queen Co	200
Harthorn Robert	Prince George Co	243
Hartwell Richard	Norfolk Co	150
Harvey George	James City Co	1425
Harvey Richard	Norfolk Co	265
Harwar Samuell	Essex Co	300
Harway Thomas	" "	1000
Harwell Samuell	Prince George Co	125

		Acres
Harwood Daniell	Accomack Co	100
Harwood Humphrey	Warwick Co	400
Harwood John	" "	704
Harwood John	Charles City Co	100
Harwood Joseph	" " "	659
Harwood Peter	Essex Co	125
Harwood Robert	Charles City Co	312
Harwood Samll	" " "	350
Harwood Thomas	Warwick Co	575
Harwood William	" "	625
Haselwood Richard	New Kent Co	100
Haskins Edward	Henrico Co	225
Haslyitt William	Elizabeth City Co	100
Hastup George	Accomack Co	300
Hatcher Benj. senr	Henrico Co	250
Hatcher Edward senr	" "	150
Hatcher Henry	" "	650
Hatcher John	" "	215
Hatcher Wm. senr	" "	298
Hatcher Wm. junr	" "	50
Hatfield Richard	James City Co	100
Hatfield William	New Kent Co	318
Hattersley Thomas	Princess Anne Co	90
Hattle Shard	Charles City Co	112
Hatton John orphans	Warwick Co	93
Hatton Samuell	" "	225
Haule Thomas	Accomack Co	500
Hawes Haughton	New Kent Co	850
Hawes Samuell	Petso-Gloucester Co	200
Hawkes Jeffrey	Prince George Co	125
Hawkins Gideon	Northampton Co	66
Hawkins John senr	" "	66
Hawkins John	James City Co	200
Hawkins John	Essex Co	1066
Hawkins Thomas	Elizabeth City Co	270
Hawkins John junr	Northampton Co	66
Hay John	Essex Co	1000
Hay William	Nansemond Co	100
Hayden John	King William Co	150
Haye Gilbert	Prince George Co	200
Hayes Adam	Princess Anne Co	1360
Hayes John	King & Queen Co	100
Hayes Peter	Isle of Wight Co	600
Hayes Robert	York Co	220
Hayes Thomas	Kingston-Gloucester Co	140
Hayes William	Norfolk Co	200
Hayes -an orphan	Petso-Gloucester Co	60
Hayfield Wm.	King William Co	100
Hayle John	King & Queen Co	685
Hayle Joseph	" " " "	250
Hayle Joseph	King William Co	200
Hayley Daniell	non-res, tax due Chas City Co	200
Haynes Nicho	Charles City Co	125
Haynes Thomas	Warwick Co	850
Haynes Thomas	King & Queen Co	494
Haywood Thomas	Ware-Gloucester Co-tax due	70

			Acres
Haywood Thomas	res. King & Queen owns	600
Hazellwood Widdo	Middlesex Co	200
Heart Thomas	Surry Co	750
Heath Adam	" "	200
Heath Adam	Prince George Co	300
Heath James	Princess Anne Co	550
Heath William	Prince George Co	320
Hemingway Mary	Abbington-Gloucester Co	150
Henderson John	Northampton Co	250
Henderson John	King & Queen (Thackers land)	200
Henderson Widdo	" " "	300
Henderson Wm	" " "	162
Hendley Charles	Princess Anne Co	100
Hendrick Hans	King William Co	700
Henland John	Norfolk Co	800
Henley John	James City Co	100
Henley Leonard	" " "	360
Herbert John	Norfolk Co	400
Herbert Thomas	" "	150
Herbert Mrs.	Prince George Co	3925
Herbert Mrs.	Henrico Co	1360
Herd Zeph.	James City Co	100
Herlock John	New Kent Co	320
Hermon Cornelius	Accomack Co	321
Herndon James.	King & Queen Co	100
Herne William	Middlesex Co	75
Herring Arthur	King & Queen Co	50
Herriott George	King William Co	200
Heslop John	Nansemond Co	148
Hester ffra.	New Kent Co	300
Hesterly John	King & Queen Co	100
Hewitt William.	Warwick Co	150
Hewitt William.	York Co	150
Heywood Henry	" "	1300
Heywood Richard	Abbington-Gloucester Co	100
Hickdon Daniell	Prince George Co	280
Hickman Henry	Accomack Co	135
Hickman John	" "	454
Hickman Roger	" "	135
Hickman Thomas	King & Queen Co	700
Hickman Thomas	King William Co. tax due	550
Hicks Richard	King & Queen Co (also sp. Hix)	250
Hife Thomas	Princess Anne Co	200
Higgason John	King William Co	350
Higgins John	James City Co	75
Hight John	New Kent Co	100
Hill Coll.	Prince George Co	1000
Hill Duke	Princess Anne Co	70
Hill Coll. Edwd	King William Co	3000
Hill Edward	Charles City Co	2100
Hill ffrancis	Northampton Co	100
Hill ffrancis	King William Co	300
Hill Gabriell	" " "	250
Hill Henry	Nansemond Co	175
Hill James	Henrico Co (tax due 50a)	795

		Acres
Hill James	Warwick Co	135
Hill John	King & Queen Co	200
Hill John	New Kent Co	250
Hill John	Prince George Co	160
Hill Leond	Essex Co	300
Hill Ralph	Prince George Co	175
Hill Richard	Petso-Gloucester Co	70
Hill Richard	Accomack Co	350
Hill Robt.	Surry Co	200
Hill Rosam'd	Henrico Co (tax due 33 ac.)	1633
Hill Madm. Tabitha	Accomack Co	3600
Hill Thomas	King William Co	150
Hill Thomas	James City Co	310
Hill Thomas	York Co	930
Hill Samll	" "	25
Hill Samll	New Kent Co	300
Hill Silvester	Isle of Wight Co	925
Hill Syon	Surry Co	300
Hill William	Nansemond Co	150
Hillard John	Warwick Co	74
Hillayres Richard	Accomack Co	300
Hilliard Jeremiah	James City Co	225
Hilliard John	" " "	200
Hilliard Thomas	Essex Co	100
Hilliard William	Abbington-Gloucester Co	80
Hilsman John	York Co	75
Hilton John	New Kent Co	300
Hind Thomas	York Co	100
Hinds Thomas	Essex Co	100
Hine Joseph	Nansemond Co	150
Hine Richard junr	" "	200
Hinman Richard	Accomack Co	1800
Hinshaw Samll	Essex Co	200
Hipkins John	Middlesex Co	100
Hitchcock John	James City Co	100
Hitchens Edward	Accomack Co	170
Hix Joseph	James City Co	100
Hix John	" " "	115
Hixs John	Prince George Co	216
Hix Robert.	" " "	1000
Hoare John.	Middlesex Co	100
Hobbs John senr	Prince George Co	250
Hobbs John	" " "	100
Hobbs Robert	" " "	100
Hobbs William	King & Queen Co	250
Hobby Laurence	Henrico Co	500
Hobday Edward	King William Co	150
Hobson William	Henrico Co	150
Hockiday Wm.	New Kent Co	300
Hockley Robert	King & Queen Co	100
Hodey Christo	Accomack Co	500
Hodge Roger	Isle of Wight Co	300
Hodges Arthur	Essex Co	100
Hodges Joseph	Norfolk Co	50
Hodges Richard	" "	375
Hodges Roger	" "	109

		Acres
Hodges Thomas	Norfolk Co	50
Hodges Thomas	King & Queen Co	250
Hodgpath John	Nansemond Co	700
Hogbin--------?	Northampton Co (non-res.)	100
Hoge Robert	Isle of Wight Co	60
Hoges John	Norfolk Co	526
Hoges Thomas	" "	407
Hogg John junr	New Kent Co	260
Hogg Mary	" " "	140
Hogg William	" " "	200
Hoggard Mr. Nath	Warwick Co	270
Hoggard Samuel	" "	120
Holcomb William	King & Queen, Bradfords land	700
Holdcroft Henry	New Kent Co	95
Holderbee William	King William Co	100
Holeman James	James City Co	150
Holland Henry	Nansemond Co	400
Holland John	" "	700
Holland Joseph	" "	100
Holland William	Ware-Gloucester Co	300
Holled Samuell	New Kent Co	100
Holliday Antho.	Isle of Wight (see Holyday)	860
Holiday Thomas	James City Co	250
Holliday William	King William Co	100
Hollier Simon	Elizabeth City Co	200
Hollingsworth Henry	Surry Co	60
Hollins John	King William Co	200
Holloman Richard	Surry Co	480
Holloman Thomas	" "	450
Holloway Edward senr.	Prince George Co	100
Holloway Edward	" " "	100
Holloway William	King & Queen Co	100
Hollowell Elener	Norfolk Co	1550
Hollowell John sr	" "	524
Hollowell John	" "	200
Hollowell Joseph	" "	1280
Hollygood Thomas	" "	100
Hollyman Christo	Isle of Wight Co	400
Hollyman Mary	Surry Co	290
Hollyman Thom	Isle of Wight Co	150
Holman orphans	Warwick Co	200
Holmes John	" "	200
Holmes Richard	Henrico Co	100
Holmes Thomas	" "	50
Holsted Henry	Norfolk Co	633
Holsted John	" "	350
Holt Elizabeth	Surry Co	1450
Holt Elizabeth	Warwick Co	150
Holt Jeremiah	Abbington-Gloucester Co	350
Holt Jeremiah jr	" " "	150
Holt John	Surry Co	150
Holt Joseph	Maryland. tax due King & Queen	321
Holt Capt. Thom	Surry Co	538
Holt William	Surry Co	630

		Acres
Holycross Joseph	Prince George Co	84
Holyday David.	York Co	600
Holyday John	Norfolk Co	440
Holyday Joseph	Nansemond Co	1000
Holy day Thomas	York Co	100
Homes Edward	Nansemond Co	300
Hoomes George	King & Queen Co	725
Honey James	" " " "	200
Hood John	James City Co	250
Hood William	Nansemond Co	200
Hood Mick.	James City Co	260
Hooker Edward	" " "	1067
Hope Capt. George	Accomack Co	900
Hopkins John	James City Co	120
Hopkins William	New Kent Co	200
Hordon William	King & Queen Co	70
Horkeey John	New Kent Co	800
Horman Robert	" " "	300
Horne Richard	Surry Co	100
Horne William	Nansemond Co	100
Horning Robert	" "	80
Horsley Richard	Elizabeth City Co	90
Horsley Rowland	New Kent Co	250
Horton Daniel	Nansemond Co	200
Hoskins Hugh	Princess Anne Co	50
Houffler Thomas	Nansemond Co	200
Hould David	Essex Co	100
Hoult Richard	" "	100
Housburrough Morris	King & Queen Co (Harts land)	200
House John	Elizabeth City Co	157
How Alexander	Petso-Gloucester Co	120
Howard Hugh	Abbington-Gloucester Co	200
Howard James	Nansemond Co	700
Howard James.	" "	25
Howard John	James City Co	25
Howard Peter	King & Queen Co	300
Howard William.	York Co	100
Howard William.	Petso-Gloucester Co	300
Howden William.	King & Queen Co	100
Howell Charles	Prince George Co	125
Howell John.	" " "	183
Howell John	Isle of Wight Co	100
Howell Thomas	" " " "	100
Howell Thomas	Prince George Co	25
Howell William	Surry Co	50
Howerton Thomas	Essex Co	175
Howerton Thomas	King & Queen Co	300
Howes Job.	New Kent Co	300
Howes Job.	King William Co., tax due	2000
Howle John	New Kent Co	150
Howle John junr	" " "	100
Howlett William.	Kingston-Gloucester Co	300
Howood James.	Charles City Co	200
Hows quarter	Essex Co	300
Hubard Richard	Petso-Gloucester Co	100
Hubberd Ralph	York Co	50

		Acres
Huberd John	New Kent Co	827
Hubert Matt.	James City Co	1834
Hubbert Robert	Warwick Co	101
Hubbert William	" "	200
Huckstep Edward	King William Co	150
Hudnell Widdo	Nansemond Co	45
Hudson George	James City Co	100
Hudson Leonard	" " "	170
Hudson Richard	Prince George Co	75
Hudson Robert	Henrico Co	281
Hudson Thomas	Essex Co	50
Hudson William	" "	300
Hudson William	" "	100
Hudson William	Accomack Co	270
Hudson William	James City Co	50
Hues Edward	Norfolk Co	1404
Hues John	Accomack Co	100
Huffington John	" "	240
Hughs Edward	Henrico Co	100
Hughes George	James City Co	250
Hughs John	New Kent Co	180
Hughes Rees	" " "	400
Hughs Robert	" " "	966
Hullett John	Norfolk Co	300
Hull Richard	Petso-Gloucester Co	250
Hunter Dr. Wm.	Princess Anne Co	80
Hunter William	Isle of Wight Co	150
Hurford Widdo	Middlesex Co	50
Hurt John	King William Co	500
Hurt Wm. senr	" " "	250
Hurt Wm. junr	" " "	90
Hurst William	Ware-Gloucester Co	200
Hutchins Garratt	Accomack Co	170
Hutchins Nicho.	Henrico Co	240
Hutchins Richard	Isle of Wight Co	300
Hutchinson Robt	Accomack Co	934
Hutchinson Wm	King William Co	600
Hutson Thomas	Essex Co	100
Hutton George	New Kent Co	150
Hyde Robert	York Co	200
Hyde William	Charles City Co	120
Hyerd Thomas	Surry Co	50
Hyne Richard	Nansemond Co	200

------- I -------

Iles John	Nansemond Co	220
Inch John	James City Co	30
Inge Vincent	King William Co	100
Inglis Mango	James City Co	1300
Inglis Mongo	York Co	400
Ingram Roger	Isle of Wight	300
Irby Edmund	Prince George Co	800
Irby Joshua	" " "	200

		Acres
Irby William	Charles City Co	103
Isaacs John Junr	Northampton Co	100
Isabell William	King William Co	150
Ives John	Norfolk Co	434
Ives Timothy	" "	400
Ives Timothy junr	" "	100
Iveson Abraham	Ware-Gloucester Co	1000
Ivey George	Norfolk Co	496
Ivey Robert	James City Co, tax due York	100
Ivie Adam	Prince George Co	200
Ivye Henry	" " "	450
Izard Fran	New Kent Co	1233

------- J -------

Jackman Jos. John Mr	Surry Co	2980
Jackson Elizabeth	James City Co	200
Jackson George	Abbington-Gloucester Co	117
Jackson George	Warwick Co	193
Jackson James	Prince George Co	80
Jackson John & Jonah	Northampton Co	625
Jackson Jonas	Accomac Co, tax due	500
Jackson Ralph	Henrico Co	250
Jackson Ralph	Prince George Co	110
Jackson Richard	James City Co	150
Jackson Robert	York Co	150
Jackson Sarah	Princess Anne Co	600
Jackson Symon	Norfolk Co	720
Jackson Thomas	Prince George Co	60
Jackson Thomas	New Kent Co	500
Jackson William	York Co	200
Jacob Abraham	Northampton Co	50
Jacob Phillip senr	" "	350
Jacob Richard	" "	200
James Henry	Elizabeth City Co	100
James Joan, widdo	Northampton Co	250
James Jonathan	Accomack Co	150
James Jonathon	King William Co	300
James John	Princess Anne Co	328
Jamison David	Essex Co	250
Jamson John	Henrico Co	225
Jaquelin Edward	James City Co	400
Jarnegan Thomas jr	Nansemond Co	165
Jarnegan Thomas	" "	600
Jarrell Thomas	Surry Co	115
Jarrett Charles	" "	615
Jarrett Fardo	" "	630
Jarrett Nich.	Prince George Co	700
Jarratt Robert	New Kent Co	1600
Jarvis Francis	Kingston-Gloucester Co	460
Javox James	Charles City Co	100
Jeeves Thomas	New Kent Co	100
Jefferson Thomas	Henrico Co, tax due on 15a	492
Jefferson Thomas	York Co	100

		Acres
Jeffes Widdo	Ware-Gloucester Co	216
Jeffrys Matt	James City Co	100
Jeffrys Richard	King & Queen Co	337
Jeffrys Thom.	James City Co	60
Jemegan Thom jr	Nansemond Co	135
Jenkins Mrs. Bridget	Elizabeth City Co	100
Jenkins David.	Essex Co	50
Jenkins Capt. Henry	Elizabeth City Co	300
Jenkins Henry	Nansemond Co	860
Jenkins John	Essex Co	93
Jenkins John	Accomack Co	400
Jenkinson Tho.	Accomack Co	374
Jennings Charles	Elizabeth City Co	225
Jennings Coll.	King William Co	4000
Jennings Edmund Esqr.	York Co	850
Jennings Edmund Esqr.	" "	1650
Jennings Edmund Esqr.	James City Co	200
Jennings Henry	Norfolk Co	100
Jenings Mary	Elizabeth City Co	250
Jennings Robert	New Kent Co	100
Jerregan Henry	Nansemond Co (see Jem, Jar)	200
Jester Francis	Accomack Co	200
Jester Samuell.	" "	200
Jester Thomas.	" "	100
Jewell Thom.	Essex Co	100
Johns Jane	King William Co	240
Johns William	" " "	100
Johnson Antho	James City Co	100
Johnson Coll	King William Co	600
Johnson Edmund	Northampton Co	400
Johnson Edward	New Kent Co	150
Johnson George	Accomack Co	200
Johnson Henry	Nansemond Co	150
Johnson Jacob	Northampton Co	350
Johnson Jacob	Princess Anne Co	1700
Johnson James	King & Queen Co	200
Johnson John senr	Northampton Co	250
Johnson John junr	" "	250
Johnson John.	James City Co	260
Johnson John.	New Kent Co	100
Johnson John.	Surry Co	350
Johnson John.	Isle of Wight Co	890
Johnson Mark	Elizabeth City Co	400
Johnson Mich.	New Kent Co	40
Johnson Capt. Obedience	Northampton Co	400
Johnson Capt. Obedience has	Accomack Co	300
Johnson Richard	Essex Co	50
Johnson Robert	Isle of Wight Co	2450
Johnson Stephen	Petso-Gloucester Co	150
Johnson Thomas senr	Northampton Co	400
Johnson Thomas junr	" "	75
Johnson Thomas	Essex Co	500
Johnson Widdo	" "	300
Johnson William	" "	650
Johnson William	Surry Co	360
Johnson William	King William Co	300

		Acres
Johnson William	New Kent Co	265
Johnson William	Accomack Co	150
Johnson Zeptha senr	Northampton Co	50
Johnson Zeptha senr with Capt Obedience Johnson	" "	250
Johnson Zeptha junr	" "	200
Johnston John	Norfolk Co	275
Johnston Mercey	" "	275
Jolef John senr	" "	840
Jolef John junr	" "	300
Joles Thomas	" "	200
Jolley Dudley	Ware-Gloucester Co	100
Jolley Thomas	Princess Anne Co	150
Jones Abraham	Isle of Wight Co	600
Jones Anne	" " "	100
Jones Arthur	" " "	900
Jones Charles	Kingston-Gloucester Co	225
Jones Edmund	Accomack Co	800
Jones Edward	Isle of Wight Co	250
Jones Elizabeth	York Co	94
Jones Evan	New Kent Co	500
Jones Evan	Princess Anne Co	600
Jones Evan	Middlesex Co	50
Jones Francis	Princess Anne Co	100
Jones Francis	New Kent Co	200
Jones ffrancis	Warwick Co	150
Jones ffrederick	King William Co	2850
Jones ffrederick	New Kent Co	500
Jones Fred	James City Co	300
Jones Henry	Prince George Co	200
Jones Hugh	Henrico Co	934
Jones Humphrey	Middlesex Co	150
Jones James senr	Prince George Co	1100
Jones James	Surry Co	1000
Jones Jane	New Kent Co	200
Jones John	" " "	100
Jones John	" " "	100
Jones John	" " "	100
Jones John	Isle of Wight Co	200
Jones John	Prince George Co	350
Jones John	Essex Co	300
Jones Matthew	Warwick Co	750
Jones Mich	Princess Anne Co	200
Jones Orlando	York Co	450
Jones Peter	Prince George Co	621
Jones Peter	Warwick Co	150
Jones Philip	Henrico Co	1153
Jones Rice	Essex Co	500
Jones Richard	" "	350
Jones Richard	Prince George Co	600
Jones Richard	Isle of Wight Co	250
Jones Richard	Accomack Co	500
Jones Richard	Princess Anne Co	200
Jones Robert	King & Queen Co	200
Jones Robert junr	" " "	130
Jones Robert	York Co	100

		Acres
Jones Robert	Prince George Co	241
Jones Roger	Middlesex Co	100
Jones Thomas	King & Queen Co	150
Jones Thomas	Accomack Co	100
Jones Thomas	Isle of Wight Co	100
Jones Thomas	" " "	700
Jones Thomas	Nansemond Co	200
Jones Walter	Essex Co	100
Jones Widdo	Abbington-Gloucester Co	45
Jones William senr	Prince George Co	600
Jones William junr	" " "	230
Jones William for Northington	Petso-Gloucester Co	530
Jones William	Ware-Gloucester Co	120
Jones William	Essex Co	165
Jones William	" "	300
Jones William	Warwick Co	70
Jones William	Nansemond Co	500
Jones William	Middlesex Co	300
Jones William	James City Co	150
Jones William	" " "	50
Jones William	York Co	70
Jones William	King & Queen Co	900
Jordan George & River	Surry Co, one tract, no one living there	
Jordan John	James City Co	1000
Jordan John	Isle of Wight Co	150
Jordan John	" " "	100
Jordan Joshua	" " "	150
Jordan Margaret	Nansemond Co	200
Jordan River & George	Surry Co, one tract, no one living there	
Jordan Robert	Nansemond Co	850
Jordan Maj. Thomas	" "	700
Jorden Benjamin	Isle of Wight Co	150
Jorden Edward	Charles City Co	100
Jorden Henry	Henrico Co	100
Jorden Matt	Isle of Wight Co	1950
Jorden Thomas	" " "	207
Jorden William	York Co	580
Joslin James	Princess Anne Co	100
Jossey Capt. James	Nansemond Co	550
Journey William	Essex Co	243
Joy Thomas	Princess Anne Co	600
Joyce John	Norfolk Co	200
Joyner Bridgeman	Isle of Wight Co	1100
Joyner Edward	Warwick Co	60
Joyner Theo	Isle of Wight Co	595
Joyner Thomas	" " "	1400
Joynes Edmund	Northampton Co	200
Joynes Major	" "	150
Judkins Samuell	Surry Co	100
Judkins William	" "	100
Jurdan George	" "	620
Jurdan Richard	" " (see Jordan)	350
Justice Ralph	Accomack Co	1050
Justis Justinian	Charles City Co	200

------- K -------

		Acres
Kaine Richard	Norfolk Co	50
Kallander Timo	King & Queen Co	100
Kavannah Arthur	Prince George Co	60
Keate William	Isle of Wight Co	200
Keble Walter	Kingston-Gloucester Co	550
Keeley George	Nansemond Co	650
Keeling Adam	Princess Anne Co	500
Keeling George	New Kent Co	1500
Keeling John	Princess Anne Co	2000
Keeling Thomas	" " "	700
Keene William	Nansemond Co	200
Keeton John	" "	2000
Kelley John orphen	Petso-Gloucester Co	150
Kelly John	Accomack Co	100
Kembro John	New Kent Co	540
Kembro John junr	" " "	150
Kemp Coll.	Kingston-Gloucester Co	200
Kemp Coll	Middlesex Co	900
Kemp James	Princess Anne Co	681
Kemp John	" " "	340
Kemp Peter	Ware-Gloucester Co	650
Kemp Peter	King William Co, tax due,	600
Kemp Richard	Middlesex Co	1100
Kemp Thomas	Kingston-Gloucester Co	200
Kemp William	Abbington-Gloucester Co	75
Kendall Richard	York Co	150
Kendall Richard	Henrico Co	400
Kendall William	Northampton Co	2410
Kendall William orphans	Accomack Co	2850
Kenniff Darby	King & Queen Co	160
Kennon Elizabeth	Henrico Co	1900
Kerle William	Nansemond Co	325
Kerney Capt. Barnaby	" "	460
Kertch Dorothy	Ware-Gloucester Co	220
Kettlerise Symon	King William Co	200
Key Robert	Essex Co	209
Kidd Thomas	Middlesex Co	250
Kigan Mary	Surry Co	200
Kilbee William	Middlesex Co	600
Killam Edward	Accomack Co	720
Killam Richard	" "	1900
Killam William	" "	450
Killingworth William	Surry Co	60
Kinder Thomas	Nansemond Co	160
Kindrick John	Ware-Gloucester Co	100
King Daniel	King & Queen Co	200
King Edward	" " "	200
King Elizabeth	New Kent Co	300
King Eusobius	Prince George Co	100
King Henry	" " "	650
King Henry	Nansemond Co	300
King John	" "	1000
King John	King & Queen Co	150

		Acres
King John	Prince George Co	50
King John	Isle of Wight Co	300
King Julian	Nansemond Co	700
King Michael	" "	80
King Robert	King & Queen Co	100
King Robert	King William Co	300
King Robert	Isle of Wight Co	300
King William	Nansemond Co	140
Kingson John	Petso-Gloucester Co	400
Kink Anne	King & Queen Co	275
Kink or Kirkland Rich	Prince George Co	300
Kirby Henry	Essex Co	60
Kirby Robert	York Co	200
Kirby Thomas	" "	270
Kitterell Jonothan	Nansemond Co	300
Kittson Richard	Accomack Co	1300
Kittson by Wm. Smith	Abbington-Gloucester Co	50
Knewstup------?	James City Co	150
Knibb Samuell	Henrico Co	209
Knibb Solomon	" "	833
Knight Henry	Kingston-Gloucester Co	240
Knight James	Nansemond Co	300
Knight John	Northampton Co	100
Knott James	Nansemond Co	1050
Knott William	Surry Co	300
Knowles Capt.	Kingston-Gloucester Co	575
Knowles Dorothy	King & Queen Co	150

------- L -------

Lacey Emanuel	New Kent Co	180
Lacey Mary	Surry Co	100
Lacey William (see Lasy)	New Kent Co	500
Lacey Thomas	New Kent Co	100
Lacy John	Essex Co	100
Ladd William	Henrico Co	70
Laforce Reu	" "	100
Lagg William	Henrico Co, tax due Chas City	100
Lailler Luke	Northampton Co	100
Lailor Francis	" " tax due Accomack	100
Lais Henry	Elizabeth City Co	100
Lamb Hannah	York Co	50
Lamb Thomas	Surry Co	200
Lambedson Abraham	Accomack Co	100
Lambkin John	Nansemond Co	50
Lancaster Robt.	Surry Co	100
Land Mr Brewer	Warwick Co	1350
Land Edward	Princess Anne Co	400
Land John Wheat	Elizabeth City Co	66
Land Lindseys	Kingston-Gloucester Co	390
Land Woodman	Warwick Co	200
Landrum James	Essex Co	100
Landrum John	" "	300

		Acres
Lane Benjamin	Abbington-Gloucester Co	50
Lane Daniell	Princess Anne Co	350
Lane Robert	Norfolk Co	460
Lane Thomas	New Kent Co	100
Lane Tho. junr	Surry Co	200
Lane Valentine	Abbington-Gloucester Co	80
La Neere George	Surry Co	300
Lang Mary	" "	70
Langford John	King & Queen Co	150
Langhorne orphans	Warwick Co	602
Langley Thomas	Norfolk Co	878
Langley William	" "	1487
Lapiter John	residence ? tax due Nansemond Co	?
Lapiter William	residence ? tax due Nansemond Co	?
Larkhum John	Nansemond Co	500
Lary James	Accomack Co	100
Lasley Patrick	Surry Co	520
Lassells Mary	Ware-Gloucester Co	200
Lassiter Robert	Nansemond Co	850
Lasy William	King William Co	100
Latham William	Elizabeth City Co	90
Latin John	York Co	150
Laton Reuben	New Kent Co	100
Lattaine Lewis	Essex Co	250
Lattimore Edward	Elizabeth City Co	190
Lattoon John	James City Co	75
Laughter John	Surry Co	300
Law James	New Kent Co	100
Law John	Essex Co	300
Lawley Patrick	Nansemond Co	50
Lawrence George	" "	400
Lawrence Henry	" "	200
Lawrence James	" "	100
Lawrence John	" "	175
Lawrence John	" "	100
Lawrence James	Charles City Co	100
Lawrence John	Northampton Co	120
Lawrence John	Isle of Wight Co	400
Lawrence Matthew	King & Queen Co	210
Lawrence Richard	James City Co	250
Lawrence Richard	Nansemond Co	200
Lawrence Robert	" "	400
Lawrence Robert	" "	130
Lawrence Robert	Isle of Wight Co	400
Lawrey James	Nansemond Co	40
Lawson Claudy	Essex Co	100
Lawson Coll H	Princess Anne Co	3100
Lawson John	York Co	100
Lawson John	New Kent Co	50
Lawson Nicho	" " "	200
Leadbeatter Francis	Prince George Co	100
Leadbeatter John	" " "	400
Leak William	New Kent Co	280
Leatherbury Chas	Accomack Co	1100

		Acres
Leatherbury Perry	Accomack Co	1750
Lee Edward	New Kent Co	120
Lee Francis	Isle of Wight Co	100
Lee Mr. Hancock, of Dividing Creeks, tax due Accomack on		4050
Lee John	King William Co	20
Lee John.	Nansemond Co	100
Lee Richard Esqr	Petso-Gloucester Co	1140
Lee Thomas	Middlesex Co	100
Lee William	York Co	350
Lee William	King & Queen Co	230
Leenein John	Prince George Co	100
Leftwich Thom	Essex Co, tax due King & Queen	75
Legatt John	Accomack Co	300
Leggett John	Princess Anne Co	400
Leigh John	King & Queen Co	6200
Lemon Elizabeth	" " " "	100
Lemon James	Princess Anne Co	1500
Lenton William	Norfolk Co	150
Lesplah Peter	New Kent Co	100
Lestrange Thomas	" " "	200
Lester Dareus	Henrico Co	100
Letts Arthur	King & Queen Co	475
Leveritt Robert	Essex Co	100
Levermore Phill	New Kent Co	1000
Leverson's quarter	Essex Co	600
Levingstone John	King & Queen Co	600
Levingstone John	" " " " on Sowell's land	750
Levingstone Samll	King & Queen Co	100
Levinia John	Norfolk Co	510
Lewelling Widdow	Warwick Co	100
Lewey Samuell	Prince George Co	100
Lewis David	King & Queen Co	120
Lewis Edward	" " " "	1400
Lewis Capt Edwd	Petso-Gloucester Co	1000
Lewis John Esqr	Abbington-Gloucester Co	2000
Lewis John Esqr	York Co	300
Lewis John Esq	King & Queen Co	10100
Lewis John Esq	New Kent Co	2600
Lewis John	" " "	375
Lewis Nicho orphan	Petso-Gloucester Co	350
Lewis Richard	Isle of Wight Co	100
Lewis Robert	Northampton Co	100
Lewis Robert	Accomac Co	200
Lewis Thom senr	Prince George Co	200
Lewis Thomas	New Kent Co	115
Lewis William	Accomack Co	300
Lewis William	" "	150
Lewis William	Henrico Co	350
Lewis Zachary	King & Queen Co	350
Liddall George	New Kent Co	100
Lidie Robert	James City Co	500
Liechfield Wm	Accomack Co	154
Liegh Hugh	Prince George Co	762
Lightfoot John Esqr	New Kent Co	3600

		Acres
Lightfoot John Esqr	New Kent Co	900
	tax due Essex Co	
Lightfoot John Esqr	James City Co	250
Lightfoot Phil.	" " "	1650
Ligon Eliza. Widdo	Henrico Co)	1341
Ligon Mary Widdo	" ")	
Ligon Hugh	" "	150
Ligon Richard	" "	1028
Lilburn Alexander	Princess Anne Co	500
Lillingtone Benj.	James City Co	100
Lindseys land	King-Gloucester Co	390
Liney William	James City Co	55
Lingoe William.	Accomack Co	300
Linsey Caleb.	Kingston-Gloucester Co	140
Linsey Joseph	New Kent Co	1150
Linsey William	" " "	50
Linton John	Warwick Co	75
Liptroll Edwd	Henrico Co	150
Little Abraham	Essex Co	60
Littlehouse Dorothy	Accomack Co	250
Littlepage Capt Richd	King William Co	2600
Littlepage Richard	New Kent Co	2160
Littleton Susannah widdo	Northampton Co	4050
Littleton South widdo.	Accomack Co	2870
Littletone John	" "	200
Livesley John	Prince George Co	300
Lobb William	King & Queen Co	100
Lochester Edwd	New Kent Co	80
Lochester Robt	" " "	80
Lockett Benjamin	Henrico Co	104
Lockett James	" "	50
Lockhart James	Nansemond Co	800
Loft Richard	King & William Co	320
Loftes Edward	Warwick Co	60
Loftin Comeles	James City Co	200
Loftin Comeles junr	" " "	200
Loftland John	Accomack Co	167
Lofton Cornelius	" "	166
Logie John	Middlesex Co	300
Logwood Thomas.	New Kent Co	100
Lomax John	Essex Co	2000
Lombrey John.	Prince George Co	400
Long Richard	Essex Co	300
Long Widdo	Isle of Wight Co	104
Longest Richard	Kingston-Gloucester Co	600
Longoe James.	Accomack Co	200
Love Elias	York Co	25
Love John	James City Co	100
Loveing John.	King & Queen Co	100
Lovegrove Richard.	Nansemond Co	150
Lovell Charles.	New Kent Co	250
Lovell George	" " "	920
Lovell Widdow	Norfolk Co	740
Loveney James	" "	100
Lovett Lancaster	Princess Anne Co	1850
Lovett Randolph	" " "	100

		Acres
Lovett Thomas	Isle of Wight Co	100
Lovett Capt Thom	res ? tax due in Nansemond Co	
Lovett William	Princess Anne Co	1300
Low Henry	Norfolk Co	191
Low Mrs. Sarah	res ? tax due Surry Co	500
Low Mrs	Prince George Co	70
Low William	" " "	1584
Lowlin Daniel	Charles City Co	600
Lownd Henry	Henrico Co	516
Lowry John for Seldon	Elizabeth City Co	110
Lowry Mr. William	" " "	526
Loyall John	York Co	100
Loyd George	Essex Co	800
Lucas Elizabeth	Warwick Co	800
Lucas Thomas	Northampton Co	100
Lucas William	Surry Co	315
Lucas William	Accomack Co	300
Ludgall Matthew	Norfolk Co	250
Ludwell Philip Coll.	Surry Co	1100
Ludwell Phil. Esqr	James City Co	6626
Luelling Edward	Norfolk Co	315
Luelling Richard	" "	200
Luke John	Northampton Co	400
	New Kent Co	150
Lumpkin Jacob	King & Queen Co	950
Lumpkin Robert	" " " "	400
Lun Arthur	York Co	50
Lund Thomas	James City Co	100
Lupo James	Isle of Wight Co	45
Lurrey Thomas	Princess Anne Co	100
Lurton Henry	Accomack Co	363
Lylley John	Kingston-Gloucester Co	584
Lynes John	York Co	150
Lynes Rebecka	King & Queen Co	405
Lyon Peter	" " " "	250
Lypscomb Ambrose	King William Co	600
Lypscomb John	" " "	200
Lypscomb William	" " "	300

------- M -------

Maberry ffrancis	Prince George Co	347
Mackay Sarah	King & Queen Co	177
Mackeny Elizabeth	New Kent Co	250
Mackenny Francis Mr	Accomack Co	5109
Macklahan Nath	Princess Anne Co	100
Macklalin John	" " "	100
Macklenny Wm	Nansemond Co	200
Macklin Wm.	James City Co	300
Mackmellion Tho.	Northampton Co	300
Mackwilliams Finley	Accomack Co	100
Mackwilliams John.	Petso-Gloucester Co	50
Mackwilliams Overton	Accomack Co	200
Maddison Henry	King William Co	650

		Acres
Madison John jr	King William Co	300
Maddison John	King & Queen Co	500
Maddox Thomas	Northampton Co	1500
Madox John	New Kent Co	300
Madox William	Prince George Co	190
Mage Peter	New Kent Co	450
Magson David	Essex Co	400
Maguffe John	" "	100
Major ffrancis	King & Queen Co	700
Major John	" " " "	400
Major John	" " " "	250
Major John	Northampton Co	390
Major John	Tax due at Occohanock on	200
Major John	James City Co	100
Major Peter	Accomack Co	113
Major Roules	" "	157
Major William	" "	130
Major William	New Kent Co	456
Malkhan Thomas	Middlesex Co	200
Mallard Poynes	James City Co	100
Mallbourn Peter	Princess Anne Co	280
Mallnote John Mr.	Warwick Co	61
Mallone Daniell	Prince George Co	100
Mallory Francis	" " "	100
Mallory Francis	Surry Co	147
Mallory Roger	King William Co	100
Mallory Thomas	" " "	150
Mallory William	Elizabeth City Co	200
Mammon Pat	Middlesex Co	100
Manders James	Charles City Co	100
Mandre Thomas	Isle of Wight Co	200
Mangann John	" " " "	100
Maning John senr.	Norfolk Co	300
Maning John junr.	" "	100
Maning Nicholas	" "	260
Maning Thomas	" "	97
Mann Robert	Henrico Co	100
Manningaren -------?	James City Co	150
Mansfield Thomas	King & Queen Co	60
Mansfield Thomas	Nansemond Co	60
Manson Peter	York Co	150
Map John	Northampton Co	50
Maples Thomas	James City Co	300
Marble George	" " "	135
Marcartee Daniell	King & Queen Co	200
Marchant Richard	Kingston-Gloucester Co	180
Marinex Hugh	Ware-Gloucester Co	50
Marinex John	" " "	100
Markham Thomas	New Kent Co	100
Marks Matt.	Prince George Co	1500
Marlor Elizabeth	Nansemond Co	80
Marr George	New Kent Co	100
Marr John	King William Co	200
Marraw Dennis	James City Co	30
Marshall George	Northampton Co	250
Marshall Humphrey	Isle of Wight Co	600

		Acres
Marshall John	Accomack Co	1666
Marshall John	Northampton Co	250
Marshall Mary	Isle of Wight Co	200
Marshall Tho. orphan	Northampton Co	75
Martin Cordelia widdo	King & Queen Co	200
Martin Elizabeth	" " " "	400
Martin Henry	Isle of Wight Co	200
Martin James	New Kent Co	100
Martin John	Prince George Co	200
Martin John	Essex Co	400
Martin John	Kingston-Gloucester Co	200
Martin John	New Kent Co	400
Martin Martin	" " "	150
Martin Richard	James City Co	150
Martin Thomas	New Kent Co	100
Martin William	" " "	230
Martin William	Princess Anne Co	200
Marston Thomas	James City Co	1000
Marston William	" " "	150
Marvell Thomas	Charles City Co	1238
Masey Peter	New Kent Co	100
Masey Thomas	" " "	300
Masnibred Roger	Elizabeth City Co	50
Mask John	New Kent Co	411
Mason Edward	Nansemond Co	150
Mason Elizabeth	Surry Co	300
Mason George	Norfolk Co	300
Mason Coll. Lemuel	Princess Anne Co	650
Mason Lemuell	Norfolk Co	400
Mason Thomas	" "	653
Mason Thomas	" "	125
Mason Thomas	Princess Anne Co	140
Mason Thomas	Nansemond Co	350
Mason widdo	Middlesex Co	100
Mastin Elizabeth	Petso-Gloucester Co	360
Matthews Baldwin	York Co	1300
Matthews Benjamin	Essex Co	200
Matthews Edward	King & Queen Co	160
Matthews Edward	Henrico Co	330
Matthews Edmd.	Surry Co	50
Matthews James	Prince George Co	100
Matthews John	Northampton Co	275
Matthews Richard	Essex Co	250
Matthews William	Accomack Co	400
Matthias Mathew	Norfolk Co	100
Matthias Mathew	Princess Anne Co	80
Mattlow James	New Kent Co	150
Maund William	Norfolk Co	200
May John	King & Queen Co	300
May John	" " " " on Pigg's land	200
May Thomas	King & Queen Co	300
Maybank Wm	King William Co	100
Mayes William	Prince George Co	763
Mayes John	" " "	365
Mayfield Robert	Essex Co	100

60

		Acres
Mayho John	Princess Anne Co	160
Mayo Valentine	Middlesex Co	100
Mayo William	Isle of Wight Co	300
McDonnell John	King William Co	150
McGehee Thomas	" " "	250
McGehe William	New Kent Co	132
McKing Alexander	" " "	170
McKoy John	" " "	300
Meachen John jr	Kingston-Gloucester Co	600
Meacon Gideon	New Kent Co	270
Mead William	King & Queen Co	100
Meanley William	New Kent Co	100
Mecoy James	Princess Anne Co	200
Medlock John	New Kent Co	350
Medor John	Essex Co	100
Medor Thomas	" "	300
Meekings Thomas	James City Co	175
Meeres William.	Accomack Co	150
Mefflin Zach.	Essex Co	400
Mellchop Elizabeth	Accomack Co	210
Mellechop Mary.	" "	498
Mellchops Nicholas	" "	285
Melo Nicholas	King & Queen Co	200
Melson John	Accomack Co	180
Melton Richard	New Kent Co	290
Mercer James	Isle of Wight Co	100
Mercer Thomas.	Norfolk Co	600
Merchant Capt. Christo.	Princess Anne Co	400
Mercy Alexander	res. Maryland, tax due Accomac Co	200
Meres Robert	res.? tax due Accomack Co	200
Merey Thomas	Warwick Co	363
Merfield John	New Kent Co	210
Meridith George.	" " "	400
Meridith James	" " "	270
Meridith Joseph.	Nansemond Co	250
Meridith Sampson.	" "	400
Merill William	Accomack Co	150
Merrett Matthew	Surry Co	60
Merrey John	Accomack Co	350
Mr. Merry or Mrs Dunn	Elizabeth City Co	500
Merriell George	Surry Co	250
Merritt John	Essex Co	100
Merritt Thomas	" "	124
Merriweather ffrancis	" "	3200
Merriweather Nicho	King William Co	600
Merriweather Nicho	New Kent Co	3327
Merriweather Thomas.	Essex Co	2100
Merse John.	" "	400
Metcalfe jno, Isaac, & Samuel	Accomack Co	600
Michaell John.	Essex Co	200
Michaell Yeardly	Northampton Co	400
Michell Grattiance	Northampton Co, Tax due in Accomac Co	200
Mickleburough Edmd	Middlesex Co	200
Mickleborough Sarah	" "	1000

		Acres
Micon Paul	Essex Co	150
Middleton George senr	Accomack Co	588
Middleton George junr	" "	150
Middleton Thomas	" "	350
Middleton Thomas	Surry Co	100
Mierick Owen	" "	250
Miggs Thomas	Kingston-Gloucester Co	100
Milbey John	Accomack Co	500
Milby Joseph	" "	830
Milby William	" "	250
Miles Daniell	King William Co	350
Miles Edward	Accomack Co	413
Miles Roger	" "	200
Miles Thomas	" "	202
Mill John	Essex Co	200
Miller John	" "	150
Miller John	Kingston-Gloucester Co	100
Miller John	Middlesex Co	200
Miller John	Norfolk Co	200
Miller Joseph	" "	882
Miller Thomas	" "	1050
Miller Widdow senr	" "	200
Miller Widdow	" "	100
Miller William	" "	1090
Millington William	New Kent Co	200
Millington Wm. junr	" " "	450
Mills Nicho	" " "	300
Milner Capt. ffrancis	Nansemond Co	479
Milner Col. Thomas	" "	1484
Milner William	Petso-Gloucester Co	900
Minge James senr	Prince George Co	500
Minge James	Charles City Co	1086
Minis Thomas	New Kent Co	200
Minor Garrett	Middlesex Co	225
Minor Minie	" "	225
Minor Richard	Petso-Gloucester Co	250
Minshea John	Isle of Wight Co	300
Minsor William	Elizabeth City Co	150
Mires Humphrey	Nansemond Co	150
Mitcham Joseph	Middlesex Co	75
Mitchell Henry	Abbington-Gloucester Co	50
Mitchell Henry senr	Prince George Co	100
Mitchell Henry junr	" " "	200
Mitchell John	Accomack Co	400
Mitchell John	Prince George Co	170
Mitchell Peter	" " "	305
Mitchell Stephen	New Kent Co	200
Mitchell Stephen junr	" " "	75
Mitchell Symon	Accomack Co	300
Mitchell Thomas junr	Prince George Co	100
Mitchell Thomas	New Kent Co	300
Mitchell William	" " "	512
Mixon John	Abbington-Gloucester Co	400
Mockey Adam	Norfolk Co	400
Mocoy Dennis, senr & junr	" "	160
Moderas Charles	Middlesex Co	100

		Acres
Mohan James	Norfolk Co	100
Mohan Warwick	New Kent Co	800
Mones Joseph	Norfolk Co	73
Mongo John	Isle of Wight Co	100
Mongo Robert	" " "	400
Montgomery Benj	Nansemond Co	910
(see names starting Mount--- ...		
Moodie Samuell	Charles City Co	82
Moody John	Essex Co	150
Moody Samuell	Prince George Co	328
Mookins Roger	James City Co	160
Moon Stephen	New Kent Co	70
Moon Thomas	" " "	65
Moon (this name could be Moor)		
Moor Anne	" " "	65
Moor Edward	" " "	65
Moor John	" " "	250
Moor Pelham	" " "	125
Moore Edward	Nansemond Co	250
Moore ffrancis	Essex Co	175
Moore George	Isle of Wight Co	400
Moore James	Nansemond Co	400
Moore John	" "	200
Moore John	" "	100
Moore Matthew	Northampton Co	175
Moore Richard	Nansemond Co	250
Moore Samuell	King & Queen Co	100
Moore Thomas	Accomack Co	166
Moore Thomas	Nansemond Co	200
Moore William	Princess Anne Co	414
More Capt. Augustine	Elizabeth City Co	285
More Austines quarter	King & Queen Co	200
More Dennis	Accomack Co	200
More Edward	" "	500
More Eliner	Northampton Co	175
More George	Ware-Gloucester Co	40
More Gilbert	Northampton Co	225
More Jacob	Princess Anne Co	200
More John	Elizabeth City Co	250
More John	Northampton Co	545
More Joseph	Abbington-Gloucester Co	150
More Richard	Prince George Co	472
More Sarah	Ware-Gloucester Co	67
More Thomas	Princess Anne Co	100
More William	" " "	100
Morecock Thom	James City Co	700
Moreing John	Surry Co	695
Mores David	James City Co	170
Morgan Edward	New Kent Co	50
Morgain John	Essex Co	100
Morgan Matthew	New Kent Co	210
Morgan Rebecca	Elizabeth City Co	50
Morgan William senr	Kingston-Gloucester Co	50
Morgan William junr	" " "	200
Moorland Edward	Surry Co	225
Morland John	York Co	100

		Acres
Morley John	Nansemond Co	100
Morrah Alexander	Princess Anne Co	200
Morrah John	" " "	200
Morraine John	Northampton Co	119
Morreigh John	New Kent Co	110
Morrin Robert	Ware-Gloucester Co	200
Morris Edward jr	James City Co	100
Moriss Henry	King & Queen Co	100
Morris Jacob	Accomack Co	200
Morriss James	Ware-Gloucester Co	250
Morris James	James City Co	800
Morris James	York Co	100
Morris John	" "	125
Morris John	Essex Co	200
Morris John	Accomack Co	640
Morris John	New Kent Co	450
Morris John	James City Co	195
Morris Josias	Princess Anne Co	900
Morris Robert	New Kent Co	245
Morris Thomas	Princess Anne Co	63
Morris William	King William Co	440
Morriss William	Ware-Gloucester Co	350
Morris William	King & Queen Co	300
Morriss William	" " "	130
Morryman James	James City Co	300
Morse Capt. ffrancis	Princess Anne Co	1300
Morse John (given Merse)	Essex Co	400
Mosely Arthur	Henrico Co	450
Moseley Benjamin	Essex Co	1100
Moseley Edward	Henrico Co	150
Mosseley Edward	Essex Co	550
Mosseley Edward senr	Princess Anne Co	1000
Moseley John	" " "	325
Mosseley Marvill	Middlesex Co	225
Mosseley Robert	Essex Co	100
Moseley Widdow	Norfolk Co	300
Moseley Capt. Wm	Princess Anne Co	600
Moseley William	" " "	50
Moss Edward	York Co	759
Moss James	New Kent Co	720
Moss John	York Co	150
Moss Robert	Essex Co	180
MMoss Samuell	New Kent Co	200
Moss Thomas	" " "	430
Moss William	Surry Co	100
Mottley John	Essex Co	100
Mountague William	Middlesex Co	500
Mountegue William	Essex Co	850
Mountford Jeffry	Charles City Co	100
Mountford Jos	York Co	307
Mountford Joseph	Warwick Co	558
Mountford Thomas	" "	890
Mountford Thomas	James City Co	600
Mountgomery Robert	Nansemond Co	150
Moxon William	New Kent Co	100
Mulick George	King & Queen Co	100

Acres

Mulleny James	Nansemond Co	500
Mullens Matthew	King William Co	150
Mullins William	Middlesex Co	150
Mulsin Edward	Princess Anne Co	100
Muncreef John	" " "	140
Munday Thomas	Essex Co	500
Munford Robert	Prince George Co	339
Murdaugh John	Nansemond Co	300
Murden Widdow	Norfolk Co	2000
Murphree James	Nansemond Co	160
Mu(r)frey Alexander	Norfolk Co	800
Murfry William	Isle of Wight Co	600
Murray Alexander	Middlesex Co	250
Murray John	Isle of Wight Co	650
Murrell Edward	Prince George Co	100
Murroho John	New Kent Co	100
Murrow Robert	Nansemond Co	320
Muscoe Salvator	Essex Co	100
Muschamp John	Charles City Co	80
Musgrove Edward	Petso-Gloucester Co	100
Mutray Thomas	New Kent Co	382
Muttlow John	James City Co	170
Myers William junr	" " "	100
Myhill John	Yorke Co	52
Myhills Mr. Edward	Elizabeth City Co	600

-------- N --------

Nagleer Sarah	Elizabeth City Co	230
Nailer William	James City Co	300
Nannaley Walter	Prince George Co	299
Napier Robert	King William Co	100
Nasareth Coll.	res. ? tax due in Norfolk Co	400
Nash Richard	Norfolk Co	100
Nash Thomas	" "	50
Nason Joshua	King & Queen Co	200
Naylor Joseph	Warwick Co	100
Naylor Thomas	Elizabeth City Co	100
Neal John	King & Queen Co	50
Neal Thomas	Petso-Gloucester Co	? ?
Neaves James	New Kent Co	150
Nedler Mr, plantacon	Warwick Co	80
Needham Thomas	Elizabeth City Co	100
Nelson Henry	King & Queen Co	440
Nelson John	Northampton Co	100
Nesham Mary, at the Blackwater, tax due James City Co		168
Netherland orphans	Prince George Co	498
Nettles Robert	Petso-Gloucester Co	300
Nevill Benjamin	Nansemond Co	475
Nevill John	Kingston-Gloucester Co	100
Nevill John	Isle of Wight Co	433
Nevill Roger	" " "	200
New Edward	Charles City Co	100
New Robert	" " "	300

Acres

Newberry William	Warwick Co	100
Newbury Nathll	Essex Co	200
Newby Nath	Nansemond Co	850
Newitt William	Surry Co	330
Newman Richard	Prince George Co	120
Newman Thomas	Isle of Wight Co	360
Newson Robert	Surry Co	250
Newson William	" "	225
Newton George	Norfolk Co	1119
Newton Henry	Essex Co	175
Newton Henry	" "	100
Newton Nicho	" "	100
Niblett Burnell	Accomack Co	100
Nicholls Elizabeth	Princess Anne Co	500
Nicholls George	Surry Co	150
Nicholls Henry	James City Co	100
Nichols Jane	Elizabeth City Co	50
Nicholls John	Middlesex Co	200
Nichols Robert	Surry Co	230
Nicholson Henry	Norfolk Co	320
Nicholson John	James City Co	144
Nicholson John	Norfolk Co	160
Nicholson William	" "	300
Nicholson William	Northampton Co	600
Nicholson William	Accomack Co	600
Nightingall John	Essex Co	100
Nixon Richard	York Co	150
Nixson Henry	Essex Co	500
Noble Mark	Warwick Co	215
Nobling Thomas	Elizabeth City Co(Archer land)	212
Nock John	Accomack Co	300
Nock William senr	Accomack Co	800
Nock William junr	" "	400
Noeway Barefoot	Surry Co	150
Nonia Richard	New Kent Co	100
Norcote Thomas	Norfolk Co	273
Norfleet Christopher	Nansemond Co	400
Norfleet Edward	" "	200
Norfleet John	" "	600
Norfleet Thomas	" "	500
Norman William	King & Queen Co	300
Norman William	Petso-Gloucester Co	150
Norment Joseph	King William Co	800
Norment Samuel	" " "	100
Norrell Hugh	James City Co	328
Norris James	King & Queen Co	100
Norris Thomas	Nansemond Co	100
Norris William	New Kent Co	100
North John	Middlesex Co	200
North William	Essex Co	900
Northern John	York Co	130
Northington by Wm. Jones	Petso-Gloucester Co	530
Northworthy Coll. George	Nansemond Co	650
Northworthy George	Isle of Wight Co	1176
Northworthy Thomas	" " "	600
Northworthy Trustram	" " "	1000

		Acres
Norton Robert	Accomack Co	1050
Norwood George	Surry Co	330
Norwood Richard	Surry Co	80
Nottingham Benja	Northampton Co	300
Nottingham Joseph	" "	150
Nottingham Richard	" "	350
Nottingham William	" "	150
Nowell Dall	Essex Co	400
Nowell Widdo	" "	300
Noyce William	King William Co	650
Nucholl James	New Kent Co	300
Nunnally Richard	Henrico Co	70
Nutting Thomas	York Co	375
Nottiboy Daniell	Isle of Wight Co	100

-------- O --------

Oadham Abraham	Nansemond Co	520
Oadham Jacob	" "	20
Oakes John	King William Co	350
Oakham John	Princess Anne Co	390
Odear John	Northampton Co	100
Odium Richard	Nansemond Co	50
Odium Thomas	" "	20
Odum John	" "	50
Odyam William	Norfolk Co	200
Ofield Alexander	Kingston-Gloucester Co	23
Ogilvie William	King & Queen Co	300
Old Edward	Princess Anne Co	450
Oliver Dorothy	Petso-Gloucester Co	130
Oliver Isaac	" " "	100
Oliver John	King William Co	140
O'Mooney Mary	James City Co	126
Onians John	Accomack Co	200
Only Clement	Northampton Co	200
Orrill Lawrence	King & Queen Co	290
Orrill William	" " "	500
Osbourn Michael	" " "	90
Osbourn Thomas	Henrico Co	288
Osbourn William	Nansemond Co	200
Osling John	New Kent Co	150
Osman James	Essex Co	300
Otey John	New Kent Co	290
Oudton Matt	" " "	190
Oustin John	King William Co	350
Outland William	Nansemond Co	400
Outlaw Edward	Norfolk Co	208
Overburry Nicho	Prince George Co	809
Overstreet James	King & Queen Co	180
	ditto at home	50
Overstreet Jeffrey	York Co	50
Overstreet Thomas	" "	50
Owen Collonell	Accomack Co	500
Owen David	Charles City Co	100

		Acres
Owen Gilbert	Nansemond Co	120
Owens Hugh	King William Co	300
Owen John	Prince George Co	25
Owens John	Princess Anne Co	190
Owens Jona	Accomack Co	230
Owen Ralph	King & Queen Co	120
Owen Thomas	Henrico Co	68
Owen William	Charles City Co	100
Owens William	Norfolk Co	650
Oxley John	Nansemond Co	100

------- P -------

Pace George	Prince George Co	1000
Pace George	" " "	246
Pace John	Middlesex Co	200
Pace Stephen	Princess Anne Co	50
Paffitt Richard	Middlesex Co	200
Page John	James City Co	1700
Page John	King William Co	1000
Page John junr	New Kent Co	400
Page John	King & Queen Co	100
Page John junr	" " "	300
Page John	York Co	490
Page Madm	Petso-Gloucester Co	550
Page Madame Mary	Abbington-Gloucester Co	3000
Page Mary Mdm	New Kent Co	3450
Page Mary	James City Co	900
Page Richard	York Co	150
Page Robert	Abbington-Gloucester Co	175
Page Thomas	Isle of Wight Co	203
Paggett Edmd	Surry Co	700
Paine Bernard	King & Queen Co	130
Paine Daniell	Northampton Co	150
Pain John	Essex Co	135
Paine Thomas	Henrico Co	300
Pait John	New Kent Co	1500
Paite Jerim	" " "	220
Pakham Ephram	Prince George Co	300
Palmer Martin	King William Co	1200
Palmer Samll	Northampton Co	1562
Pall William	James City Co	450
Pallett Mathew	Princess Anne Co	600
Pamplin Nicholas	Ware-Gloucester Co	210
Pamplin Robert	King & Queen Co	150
Pann John	" " "	200
Pardoe Ph:	Isle of Wight Co	100
Parish Abraham	Elizabeth City Co	100
Parish Charles	Charles City Co	100
Parish Edward	" " "	100
Parish Guy	Petso-Gloucester Co	100
Parish John	Charles City Co	100
Parish John	Elizabeth City Co	50
Parish Joseph-res. Kiquotan	tax due Chas. City Co	100

		Acres
Parish Mark	Elizabeth City Co	200
Parish Thomas	James City Co	100
Parish William	Charles City Co	100
Park Coll	New Kent Co tax due on	7000
Park Daniell esqr	York Co	2750
Park Daniell esqr	James City Co	1800
Parkes Coll	King William Co	4500
Park John	New Kent Co	200
Park John junr	" " "	300
Park Mary	Surry Co	100
Parks James	King & Queen Co	200
Parker Francis	Nansemond Co	170
Parker Francis	Isle of Wight Co	210
Parker Capt. George	Accomack Co	2609
Parker James	Charles City Co	160
Parker John	Essex Co	250
Parker Nich senr	Henrico Co	500
Parker Peter	Nansemond Co	140
Parker Phillip	Accomack Co	150
Parker Richard	Surry Co	269
Parker Richard	Nansemond Co	514
Parker Thomas	Charles City Co	1667
Parker Thomas	James City Co	1650
Parker Thomas	Nansemond Co	100
Parker Thomas	" "	300
Parker William	" "	140
Parker William	" "	100
Parker William	Henrico Co	100
Parker William	Accomack Co	362
Parnell John	Isle of Wight Co	400
Parramore Thomas	Northampton Co	400
Parriott Mich	Kingston-Gloucester Co	100
Parrott Lawrence	" " "	340
Parsons John	Isle of Wight Co	155
Parsons Wm. orphen	Petso-Gloucester Co	100
Pasley Robert	New Kent Co	300
Pasmore George	Prince George Co	330
Passones John	Elizabeth City Co	780
Pasque Peter	York Co	12
Pate John of Gloucester	King & Queen Co owns	1000
Pate John of Gloucester	Petso-Gloucester Co	1000
Patterson William	Accomack Co	200
Pattison Alex	James City Co	100
Pattison Catherine	" " "	150
Pattison David	New Kent Co	300
Pattison Joseph	Henrico Co	500
Pattison Joseph	Prince George Co	200
Pattison Robert	Norfolk Co	350
Pattison Thomas	James City Co	200
Pattram Fra.	Henrico Co	778
Paulin Elizabeth	King & Queen Co	175
Paulmer James	York Co	150
Payne Widdo	Essex Co	1000
Paytons quarter	King & Queen Co	500
Peale Robert	Nansemond Co	275
Peale William	" "	180

		Acres
Pearce Peter	Elizabeth City Co	50
Pearce Samuell	" " "	100
Pearce William	Norfolk Co	100
Pearman John	James City Co	200
Pearman Wm	" " "	270
Pearse Phill	Isle of Wight Co	500
Pease John	New Kent Co	100
Pee Thomas	King William Co	400
Peek John	" " "	100
Peice John	Henrico Co	130
Peirce Francis	" "	312
Peirce William	" "	175
Pekithman Wm	York Co	650
Pemberton George	King William Co	180
Pemberton Thomas	King & Queen Co	115
Pender Paul	Nansemond Co	200
Pender Paul	" "	240
Pendexter George	New Kent Co	1490
Pendexter Thomas	New Kent Co	1000
Pendexter Thomas	James City Co	550
Pendleton Henry	King & Queen Co	700
Pendleton Philip	" " "	300
Penix Edward	New Kent Co	200
Penny Bryan	Elizabeth City Co	50
Penny John	Isle of Wight Co	300
Peoples David	Prince George Co	60
Peoples Elizabeth	" " "	235
Peoples William	" " "	150
Peper Stephen	James City Co	100
Perkins Charles	" " "	320
Perkins Henry	Essex Co	300
Perkins John	New Kent Co	120
Perkins Wm.	" " "	305
Perkins Wm.	Norfolk Co	50
Perkinson John	Henrico Co	622
Perkinson Seth	" "	50
Perrin Ann	" "	500
Perrott Henry	Middlesex Co	1100
Perrott Richard	Kingston-Gloucester Co	35
Perry Grace	Prince George Co	100
Perry John	Nansemond Co	870
Perry John	Accomack Co	217
Perry Joseph	Princess Anne Co	35
Perry Joseph	Prince George Co	275
Perry Micajah	" " "	600
Perry Nicho	Nansemond Co	200
Perry Samll	Essex Co	225
Perry Thomas	Princess Anne Co	650
Perry Thomas	Accomack Co	232
Persons James	York Co	350
Persons John	" "	300
Persons John	Surry Co	830
Pervine Lewis	Princess Anne Co	800
Peteras Thomas	Essex Co	200
Peters Elizabeth	Nansemond Co	334
Peters James	" "	340

Acres

Peters Mr. James	Princess Anne Co	889
Peters John	Nansemond Co	368
Peters Robert	York Co	160
Peters Thomas	Kingston-Gloucester Co	30
Peters Widdow	Norfolk Co	698
Petever Thomas	New Kent Co	100
Petterson John	Prince George Co	428
Petterson John	" " "	373
Pettfort John	Surry Co	200
Pettfort Wm	" "	50
Pettit Thomas	King & Queen Co	548
Pettman Obedience	Accomack Co	115
Pettoway Elizabeth	Surry Co	650
Pettus John	King & Queen Co, tax	
	due Essex Co	800
Petty John	New Kent Co	2190
Petty Stephen	" " "	200
Pew Henry	Henrico Co	350
Peyton Robert	Kingston-Gloucester Co	680
Peyton Thomas	" " "	684
Phelps Humphrey	Surry Co	100
Phelps Thomas	King & Queen Co	400
Phillip Charles	" " " "	250
Phillps Edward	James City Co	100
Philip George	New Kent Co	100
Phillips John	James City Co	300
Phillips John	Surry Co	270
Phillips Nathaniel	Prince George Co	150
Phillips Nicholas	York Co	150
Phillips William	Surry Co	300
Phillips William	Accomack Co	200
Philips William	James City Co	300
Philpot Richard	Norfolk Co	200
Phinkett Elizabeth	King & Queen Co	500
Pickett John	Essex Co	800
Pickles Thomas	King & Queen Co	93
Pickley Thomas	New Kent Co	281
Pickrell Gabriell	King William Co	100
Pierce Matt.	York Co	100
Pierce Phillip	Isle of Wight Co	500
Pierce Widdow	Warwick Co	155
Pigeon Richard	Prince George Co	524
Pigg Edward	King & Queen Co	250
Pigg Henry	" " " "	61
Pigg John	" " " "	100
Pigot Benj	James City Co	90
Piggott Ralph	Northampton Co	1368
Pinkitt John	Henrico Co	215
Pinkitt Thomas	" "	300
Pinkitt William	" "	192
Pipkin John	Nansemond Co	100
Pisburn John	Princess Anne Co	314
Piskell John	Essex Co	300
Pitt Henry	Isle of Wight Co	700
Pitt John	" " " "	3400
Pitt Thomas	" " " "	300

		Acres
Pittett John	Northampton Co	275
Pittett Justian.	" "	200
Pittett Thomas	" "	300
Pittlader Tho.	New Kent Co	295
Pittlader William	" " "	147
Pittman Thomas junr	Surry Co	100
Pitts John	Essex Co	200
Pitts Robert.	Accomack Co	2300
Plantine Peter.	New Kent Co	240
Pleasants John	Henrico Co	9669
Pleasants Joseph	" "	1709
Pledge John	" "	100
Pley Widdow	Essex Co	800
Plumer Isaac	Kingston-Gloucester Co	200
Plumer Thomas.	" " "	400
Plummer Wm.	" " "	510
Poe Samuell	Essex Co	800
Polland Henry	Henrico Co	235
Polland Thom senr	" "	130
Polland Thom junr	" "	235
Pollard Robert.	King & Queen Co	500
Pollard William	" " " "	100
Pollard William	King William Co	500
Pomea ffrancis	King & Queen Co	100
Pond John.	York Co	112
Pond Stephen	" "	200
Poole George	Princess Anne Co	1085
Poole Thomas.	Ware-Gloucester Co	600
Poole Thomas.	Elizabeth City Co	1200
Pope Henry.	Isle of Wight Co	557
Pope John	" " " "	250
Pope William.	Nansemond Co	890
Porter John	" "	450
Porter John	New Kent Co	100
Porter John.	Henrico Co	100
Porter Samuell	Norfolk Co	100
Porter William	Henrico Co	305
Porteus John	Isle of Wight Co	100
Porteus Madm	Petso-Gloucester Co	500
Porteus Robert.	" " "	892
Portous John	Isle of Wight Co	300
Portlock ----- ?	Norfolk Co	360
Portlock Elizabeth	Henrico Co	1000
Potter Frances widdo	King & Queen Co (Neal land)	100
Potter John	York Co	93
Potter Joseph.	" "	25
Potts Thomas.	Prince George Co	200
Pounce George	Accomack Co	400
Powell Frances widdo	Northampton Co	1225
Powell Honor	Essex Co	72
Powell Isaac	York Co	100
Powell Lemuell	Norfolk Co	246
Powell John	Northampton Co	637
Powell John	Nansemond Co	758
Powell Mark	Princess Anne Co	550
Powell Mark	Elizabeth City Co	184

		Acres
Powell Place	Essex Co	72
Powell Richard	Norfolk Co	100
Powell Robert	Henrico Co	150
Powell Robert	King & Queen Co	500
Powell Samuel	Northampton Co	200
Powell Seymor	Warwick Co	250
Powell Seamor	York Co	130
Powell Thomas	Essex Co	72
Powell Thomas	Ware-Gloucester Co	460
Powell Thomas	Isle of Wight Co	100
Powell Widdo	" " " "	480
Powell William	" " " "	200
Powell William	Essex Co	72
Powell William	Norfolk Co	624
Powers Charles.	Elizabeth City Co	400
Powers David.	King William Co	200
Powers Edward.	Warwick Co	200
Poythres Francis senr	Prince George Co	1283
Poythres Jno. junr	" " "	916
Poythres Thomas.	" " "	616
Pratt John	Accomack Co	50
Preeday Daniell	Elizabeth City Co	50
Prescott Moses	Norfolk Co	1200
Preson Thomas	Northampton Co	600
Preson Thomas . . . . owns	Accomack Co	200
Presser John	Essex Co	450
Preston Henry	Kingston-Gloucester Co	1500
Prewitt William.	King & Queen Co	200
Price Edward.	Nansemond Co	140
Price Elizabeth.	" "	150
Price John.	Middlesex Co	519
Price John.	Prince George Co	50
Price John	Ware-Gloucester Co	600
Price John	Essex Co	1100
Price John	Surry Co	340
Price Richard.	Petso-Gloucester Co	600
Price Richard.	Accomack Co	100
Price William.	Essex Co	100
Pride Wm. senr	Henrico Co	1280
Priest James	Elizabeth City Co	50
Priest James	Warwick Co	50
Prince George	James City Co	50
Pritchett David	King & Queen Co	225
Pritchett John	Petso-Gloucester Co	850
Pritchett Joseph	Prince George Co	50
Pritchett Roger	Essex Co	167
Proctor Joshua	Surry Co	660
Proctor Rubin	Isle of Wight Co	250
Pryan William	" " " "	200
Pryor Christo	King & Queen Co	175
Pryor Robert	Ware-Gloucester Co	300
Pugh Anne	Nansemond Co	2300
Pullam William.	New Kent Co	575
Pully William.	Surry Co	300
Pulystone John	" "	1400
Purcell Arthur	Isle of Wight Co	750

		Acres
Purchase George	King & Queen Co	580
Purdy Nicholas	New Kent Co	200
Purlevant Arthur	King William Co	100
Purly John	New Kent Co	100
Purnell Thomas	Ware-Gloucester Co	163
Putman Thomas	Kingston-Gloucester Co	300
Pyke Henry	Northampton Co	150
Pynes Natheniel	King William Co	1400
Pyraul James	New Kent Co	150
Pywell Charles	Accomack Co	150

------- Q -------

Quarles Dyley	King & Queen Co (Zach Lewis' land)	300
Quarles James	King & Queen Co	300
Quarles John	King William Co	100

------- R -------

Rabey Adam	Nansemond Co	586
Rabishaw Wm	Northampton Co	55
Rachell George	Surry Co	70
Rachell William	Prince George Co	100
Radford William	Ware-Gloucester Co	200
Raglin Evan	New Kent Co	300
Raglin Evan junr	" " "	100
Raglin Thomas	" " "	100
Ragsdale Godfrey	Henrico Co	450
Ramsey Thomas	Essex Co	550
Randall Giles	Norfolk Co	150
Randall John	King William Co	100
Randolph Capt. Henry' orphans by Capt. Giles Webb	Prince George Co, tax due	129
Randolph Coll.	" " "	226
Randolph Col. Wm	Henrico Co, inc1185 Swamp ld,	9465
Randolph Col. Wm	Surry Co	1655
Randolph Widdo	New Kent Co	100
Ranshaw Samuel	Warwick Co	238
Ranshaw Sarah	" "	125
Ransom Coll. James	Kingston-Gloucester Co	1400
Ransom James junr	" " "	310
Ransom Peter	Essex Co	1200
Ransom Peter quarter	" "	300
Ransome Peter	Ware-Gloucester Co	220
Rany Robert	Princess Anne Co	70
Rascow Arthur	Northampton Co	100
Rascow Mr's orphans	Warwick Co	1195
Ratcliff Nathaniel	Accomack Co	300
Ratcliff Richard	Isle of Wight Co	380
Raules John	Nansemond Co	600

		Acres
Rawlett Peter	Henrico Co	164
Raye Francis	Prince George Co	300
Ray James	King William Co	100
Ray John	Ware-Gloucester Co	100
Rayford Phillip	Isle of Wight Co	650
Raymond James	New Kent Co	80
Rayner Francis	Isle of Wight Co	80
Reace Roger senr	Prince George Co	100
Reace Roger junr	" " "	100
Read Benjamin	Kingston-Gloucester Co	550
Read Elizabeth	King & Queen Co	550
Read Henry	Prince George Co	75
Read Henry	Accomack Co	350
Read John	" "	200
Read John	Warwick Co	875
Read Robert	York Co	750
Read Thomas	Ware-Gloucester Co	400
Read Thomas	Petso-Gloucester Co	2000
Read Thomas	Northampton Co	150
Read William	Surry Co	150
Read William	" "	450
Readich George	Isle of Wight Co	790
Reading Timothy serr	Prince George Co	460
Reanes William	" " "	250
Reazon Frances	Surry Co	200
Recetts Michaell	Accomack Co (Reddick)	300
Reddick Abraham	Nansemond Co	400
Reddick Capt James	Nansemond Co	943
Reddick John	" "	300
Reddick Robert	" "	200
Redford John	Henrico Co	775
Redwood John	New Kent Co	1078
Reeks John	Prince George Co	50
Reeves James	Essex Co	200
Reeves Joseph	" "	200
Reeves Thomas	Isle of Wight Co	600
Renthall Joseph	Charles City Co	270
Revell John	Accomack Co	1450
Revis William	James City Co	150
Rews John	'not in Va.' tax due	
	Northampton Co	100
Reynolds Elizabeth	Surry Co	150
Reynolds Elizabeth	Isle of Wight Co	100
Reynolds James senr	Essex Co	500
Reynolds James	" "	500
Reynolds James	Petso-Gloucester Co	200
Reynolds James	Warwick Co	75
Reynolds Jonah	New Kent Co	50
Reynolds Richard senr	Isle of Wight Co	853
Reynolds Richard	" " "	746
Reynolds Richard	Middlesex Co	50
Reynolds Robert	Surry Co	150
Reynolds Samuell	New Kent Co	820
Reynold. Thomas	" " "	255
Reynolds William	King William Co	100
Reyley John	New Kent Co	100

Acres

Reyley Thomas	Accomack Co	225
Rhoads Charles	New Kent Co	175
Rhodes Ezekiah	Middlesex Co	300
Rhodes Frances	James City Co	100
Rhodes Nicholas	King William Co	150
Rhodes Randall	James City Co	50
Ribs Henry	Essex Co	400
Rice ffrancis orphans	Warwick Co	200
Rice John	Nansemond Co	140
Rice Michaell	King & Queen Co	200
Rice Thomas	Kingston-Gloucester Co	34
Richards Alexander	Accomack Co	150
Richards Eman	New Kent Co	1250
Richards John	King & Queen Co	914
Richards Lettis	Northampton Co	150
Richards Oliver	King & Queen Co	250
Richards Robert	Isle of Wight Co	450
Richards Robert	" " "	100
Richards Robert	King & Queen Co	300
Richards William	" " "	400
Richards Wm. in Pamunkey	Petso-Gloucester Co	150
Richardson Edward	Prince George Co	300
Richardson Elizabeth	Abbington-Gloucester Co	500
Richardson Henry	New Kent Co	300
Richardson John	" " "	1450
Richardson John	Isle of Wight Co	150
Richardson John	Princess Anne Co	1000
Richardson Joseph	Surry Co	300
Richardson Matt	New Kent Co	200
Richardson Richard	" " "	890
Richardson Robert	Essex Co	200
Richardson Thomas	Norfolk Co	379
Richeson Elias	King & Queen Co	180
Richeson Peter	Abbington-Gloucester Co	250
Richeson Thomas	King & Queen Co	460
Richmond Robert	Princess Anne Co	1000
Ricks Isaac	Isle of Wight Co	700
Ridley Garrett	Warwick Co	300
Ridley Natt	Isle of Wight Co	200
Riddle Tho for Read's Land	King & Queen Co	700
Rigdall John	Essex Co	300
Riners John	Prince George Co	200
Ring's quarter	King & Queen Co	1000
Ripley Andrew	Kingston-Gloucester Co	40
Rispus Christopher	" " "	200
River Edward	Warwick Co	375
Rivers Robt. for Morris Fallihan's orphans	Prince George Co tax	200
Roach John senr	Charles City Co	630
Road John	Accomack Co	110
Roades Charles	Nansemond Co	800
Roades Henry	" "	100
Roads Thomas	" "	75
Roane William	Petso-Gloucester Co	500
Roatton Richard	Elizabeth City Co	50
Roberts Benjamin	Princess Anne Co	100

76

		Acres
Roberts Charles	Nansemond Co	50
Roberts Edmund	Essex Co	300
Roberts Edward	Nansemond Co	250
Roberts Francis	Accomack Co	200
Roberts George	Kingston-Gloucester Co	170
Roberts John	Essex Co	50
Roberts John	Isle of Wight Co	950
Roberts John	Prince George Co	316
Roberts John	Northampton Co	200
Roberts Joseph	Norfolk Co	100
Roberts Mary	York Co	25
Roberts Maurice	King William Co	200
Roberts Obedience	Northampton Co	260
Roberts Richard for his wife	Abbington-Gloucester Co	300
Roberts Robert	Warwick Co	60
Roberts Samuell	Norfolk Co	800
Roberts Thomas	York Co	450
Roberts Thomas	Elizabeth City Co	250
Roberts Thomas	Nansemond Co	30
Robertson George	Henrico Co	1445
Robertson John	" "	415
Robertson Thomas	" "	200
Robins Edward	Accomack Co	782
Robins Majr. John	" "	2700
Robins Majr. John	Northampton Co	1180
Robins John	Ware-Gloucester Co	900
Robins Littleton	Northampton Co	1000
Robins William	Accomack Co	200
Robinson Anthony	York Co	183
Robinson Benjamin	Northampton Co	250
Robinson Christo.	Middlesex Co	4000
Robinson Christo's quarter	Essex Co	2200
Robinson Daniel	King & Queen Co	100
Robinson George	Warwick Co	70
Robinson George	Petso-Gloucester Co	300
Robinson Henry	Elizabeth City Co	200
Robinson John	Middlesex Co	1350
Robinson John, son of Robt.	King & Queen Co, nobody Pays	750
Robinson Jonothan	Nansemond Co	400
Robinson Lieut-Coll	Accomack Co	600
Robinson Nathaniel	Prince George Co	100
Robinson Robert	King & Queen Co	980
Robinson Mr. Tully	Princess Anne Co	500
Robinson William	Elizabeth City Co	50
Rodgers John	Accomack Co	100
Rodgers Richard	" "	450
Roe Edward	Elizabeth City Co	100
Rogers Benjamin	Nansemond Co	600
Rogers Francis	Elizabeth City Co	200
Rogers Giles	King & Queen Co	475
Rogers John	Isle of Wight Co	200
Rogers John	York Co	650
Rogers John	Nansemond Co	200
Rogers Joseph	" "	15
Rogers Peter	Accomack Co	167

Acres

Rogers Robert	Nansemond Co	300
Rogers Thomas	" "	50
Rogers William	Accomack Co	200
Rogers William	Surry Co	450
Rohings William	" "	596
Rollings Gregory	" "	106
Rollings Peter	King & Queen Co	150
Ronan William	Northampton Co	150
Roper John	Charles City Co	220
Rose John	Norfolk Co	60
Rose Richard	Surry Co	100
Rose Robert	Norfolk Co	385
Rose Thomas	Accomack Co	7
Ross Andrew	Nansemond Co	150
Ross William	New Kent Co	150
Rouch Rachell	Henrico Co	300
Roundtree John	Nansemond Co	475
Roundtree Robert	" "	245
Roundtree Thomas	" "	350
Roundtree William	New Kent Co	100
Rovell John	James City Co	50
Row James	Abbington-Gloucester Co	300
Row William	York Co	902
Rowe John	King & Queen Co	100
Rowen ffrancis	Henrico Co	148
Rowles John	Accomack Co	650
Rowles Wm. orphans	Warwick Co	150
Rowlett William	Henrico Co	200
Rowling John	Surry Co	476
Rowze Edward	Essex Co	300
Rowze Ralph	" "	610
Roy Richard	King & Queen Co	1600
Royal Capt. Henry	Elizabeth City Co	750
Royall Henry	Warwick Co	246
Royall Joseph	Henrico Co	783
Royall Joseph	Charles City Co	262
Royley Sarah	Accomack Co	150
Royston John	Essex Co	1000
Royston John	Petso-Gloucester Co	570
Rucker Peter	Essex Co	500
Ruffice Elizabeth	Surry Co	3001
Rule Widdow	New Kent Co	50
Russell Alexander	King & Queen Co	400
Russell Charles	Henrico Co	200
Russell John	" " 23 acres tax due	93
Russell John	Princess Anne Co	300
Russell John	" " "	150
Russell John	New Kent Co	550
Russell Joseph	Warwick Co	150
Russell Nathaniel	Abbington-Gloucester Co	550
Russell Samuell	James City Co	350
Russell Samuell	Charles City Co	253
Rutter John	Isle of Wight Co	300
Rutter John	Nansemond Co	80
Rutter Thomas	" "	75
Rutter William	" "	75

78

		Acres
Ryder Mary	James City Co	350
Ryland Thomas	Kingston-Gloucester Co	272
Ryley Elias	King & Queen Co	200

-------- S --------

Sadler Edward	Kingston-Gloucester Co	20
Sadler John	Abbington-Gloucester Co	125
Sadler Robert	Kingston-Gloucester Co	50
Sail Cornelius	Essex Co	73
Sales Widdo	" "	1150
Sall Stephen	Princess Anne Co	250
Salmon James	Prince George Co	477
Salmon John	Essex Co	60
Salmon Thomas	New Kent Co	50
Sammons John	Princess Anne Co	150
Sampson James	Isle of Wight Co	1200
Sampson Widdo	Charles City Co	211
Samll Anthony	Essex Co	300
Samll Thompson	" "	1300
Sandbourne Daniall	Isle of Wight Co	180
Sandbourne William	Prince George Co	40
Sanders Eustick	Northampton Co	100
Sanders Francis	Isle of Wight Co	100
Sanders Henry	" " "	700
Sanders James	New Kent Co	60
Sanders John	" " "	130
Sanders John	James City Co	50
Sanders John	Nansemond Co	150
Sanders John	" "	165
Sanders John Mr.	Princess Anne Co	203
Sanders John	Essex Co	300
Sanders Mr. John	York Co	100
Sanders Joshua	King William Co	100
Sanders Nathaniell	King & Queen Co	200
Sanders Richard	Northampton Co	100
Sanders Richard	Nansemond Co	500
Sanders Richard	" "	100
Sanders Thomas	Abbington-Gloucester Co	450
Sanders Thomas	New Kent Co	25
Sanders William	" " "	40
Sanders William	Nansemond Co	200
Sanders William junr	Nansemond Co	165
Sanderson John	Northampton Co	636
Sandever John	York Co	100
Sandford Samuell	Accomack Co	3250
Sandford Sarah	Princess Anne Co	1200
Sandidge John	New Kent Co	100
Sandlan Nicholas	King William Co	700
Santo Robert	James City Co	100
Satterwhite Charles	King William Co	150
Satterwight John	Abbington-Gloucester Co	50
Sarrazin Stephen	Henrico Co	120
Savage Charles	Surry Co	358

Acres

Savage Griffen	Accomack Co	650
Savage Henry	Surry Co	200
Savage John senr	Accomack Co	350
Savage Mary	Surry Co	263
Savage Rouland senr	Accomack Co	950
Savage Thomas	Northampton Co	450
Savage Thomas	Accomack Co	450
Savage William	" "	150
Savage William	Prince George Co	150
Savidge Elkington	Northampton Co	750
Savidge John	" "	410
Savidge Capt. Thomas	" "	1600
Savoy Francis	Elizabeth City Co	50
Sawer's Peter orphans	Warwick Co	95
Sawrey John	King & Queen Co	113
Sawyer Thomas	Nansemond Co	180
Sawyer William	Abbington-Gloucester Co	150
Sayer Francis	Norfolk Co	600
Scagin John	Surry Co	100
Scandlin Denis	King & Queen Co	1470
Scarbrough Majr. Bennitt	Accomack Co	521
Scarbrough Charles	" "	1000
Scarbrough Edmund Coll	" "	2000
Scarbrough Mrs Elizabeth	" "	4205
Scarbro. Edward	Surry Co	150
Scarsbrook John	Warwick Co	850
Scarborow William	Middlesex Co	200
Sclator Richard	Nansemond Co	300
Scoking Richard	Prince George Co	100
Scot David	Northampton Co	300
Scot George	" "	100
Scot Henry	" "	800
Scot John	" "	100
Scot William senr	" "	153
Scott David	Princess Anne Co	600
Scott John	Prince George Co	300
Scott John	New Kent Co	300
Scott Robert	Isle of Wight Co	300
Scott Thomas	Norfolk Co	400
Scott Thomas	Accomack Co	100
Scott Thomas	Princess Anne Co	100
Scott Walter	Henrico Co	550
Scott William	Essex Co	1100
Scrugg John	New Kent Co	50
Scrugg Richard	" " "	100
Seudy Anthony or Seady	Northampton Co	120
Seager Oliver	Middlesex Co	380
Seamore John	Northampton Co	200
Seamour William	King & Queen Co	268
Seat Joseph	Surry Co	295
Seaton Henry	Abbington-Gloucester Co	170
Seawell Thomas	" " "	200
Sebrell Nicholas	York Co	150
Sebrill Anthony	" "	50
Sebrill John	King & Queen Co	130
See Matthew	King William Co	200

		Acres
Sellers Jacob	King William Co	350
Selloway John	Isle of Wight Co	900
Selman Henry	Accomack Co	180
Selvey Jacob	James City Co	50
Serginton John	York Co	150
Servant Mr. Berthram	Elizabeth City Co	418
Sesoms Nicholas	Surry Co	800
Seveaker James	Prince George Co	710
Sevill William	Nansemond Co	85
Sewards Anne	Surry Co	300
Sewell John	James City Co	75
Sewell William	Henrico Co	59
Sewins Thomas	Surry Co	400
Sexton William	New Kent Co	80
Sexton William	Prince George Co	50
Shackelfield James	Ware-Gloucester Co	35
Shackelford Francis	Essex Co	300
Shackelford Henry	" "	50
Shackelford John	Petso-Gloucester Co	280
Shaley John	James City Co	150
Sharp Francis	York Co	100
Sharp John	James City Co	800
Sharp Robert	Henrico Co	500
Sharp Thomas	Surry Co	70
Sharples Henry	Norfolk Co	100
Shea Luke	Nansemond Co	650
Shea Patrick	King & Queen Co	200
Shears Paul	New Kent Co	200
Sheene Francis	Princess Anne Co	300
Sheffield Martin	Prince George Co	150
Sheldon William	York Co	750
Shepard Isaac	King & Queen Co	100
Shepherd Izraell	Nansemond Co	200
Shepherd Jeremiah	Essex Co	300
Shepherd John	Elizabeth City Co	210
Shepherd Joseph	King & Queen Co	100
Shepherd John	Northampton Co	200
Shepherd Thomas	" "	140
Shepherd Widdo	" "	830
Shepherd William	Accomack Co	200
Sherland John	Princess Anne Co	800
Sherman Elizabeth	James City Co	500
Sherrer John	Isle of Wight Co	200
Sherrer Thomas	" " "	200
Sherriff Henry	New Kent Co	100
Sherwood James	Princess Anne Co	200
Shield Delight	Accomack Co	300
Shields Robert	York Co	400
Shilling George	King William Co	300
Ship Joseph	Essex Co	350
Ship William	Princess Anne Co	300
Shipley John	Essex Co	200
Shipley Ralph	Kingston-Gloucester Co	430
Shoehorn Cornelius	York Co	100
Shoot Thomas	King & Queen Co	100
Short John	James City Co	90

Short Thomas	Essex Co	150
Short William	Surry Co	400
Shottwater Benj	York Co, tax due James City Co	300
Shrowsbury Francis	Surry Co	820
Shrowsbury Joseph	" "	260
Shrowsbury Thomas	" "	566
Shuckelford Roger	King & Queen Co	250
Shurly Richard	Middlesex Co	200
Sickes John	Norfolk Co	200
Sickes Walter senr	" "	550
Sill William	Accomack Co	200
Silverthorn Sebastian	" "	150
Silverthorn William	" "	160
Silvester Richard	Norfolk Co	1280
Simes William	James City Co	650
Simkins Anne	Accomack Co	1000
Simmons Mary (see Sum or Sy)	Elizabeth City Co	200
Simons Samuell	Ware-Gloucester Co	120
Simpson Thomas	Accomack Co	520
Simpis Charles	King & Queen Co	100
Sims George	Surry Co	200
Sims John	New Kent Co	1000
Sincocke John	Accomack Co	125
Singleton Henry	Kingston-Gloucester Co	600
Singleton Robert	" " "	650
Singleton Samuell	" " "	300
Sinch Widdo	" " "	300
Sivepson Thomas	Petso-Gloucester Co	280
Skelton John	King & Queen Co	100
Skerin Widdo	Henrico Co	75
Sketto Edward	Nansemond Co	200
Sketto Francis	" "	100
Sketto Isaac	" "	100
Skinner John	Elizabeth City Co	50
Skipwith Sir William	Middlesex Co	350
Skipwith Sir William	King & Queen Co, not paid for	700
Slade William	James City Co	80
Slater James	New Kent Co	700
Slaughter George	King William Co	100
Slaughter Henry	" " "	100
Slaughter James	York Co	250
Slaughter John	King William Co	90
Slaughter Martin	" " "	130
Slaughter Phoebe	Essex Co	352
Slaughter Richard	York Co	275
Small Benjamin	Nansemond Co	100
Small John	" "	100
Smallpage Robert	James City Co	190
Smart Matthew	Prince George Co	100
Smaw John	Northampton Co	800
Smell Matthew	Elizabeth City Co	100
Smelly Lewis	Isle of Wight Co	550
Smelley Robert	" " "	600
Smelley William	" " "	280
Smelt Mr. William	Elizabeth City Co	150

		Acres
Smith Abraham	Northampton Co	300
Smith Alexander	King & Queen Co	275
Smith Arthur	Isle of Wight Co	3607
Smith Augustin jr	Petso-Gloucester Co	500
Smith Augustin	" " "	200
Smith Austin in Gloucester	Tax due King & Queen Co on	4000
Smith Benjamin	Elizabeth City Co	650
Smith Captain	Kingston-Gloucester Co	550
Smith Charles	Essex Co	3000
Smith Christo	King & Queen Co	200
Smith Christo	King William Co	800
Smith Christo	James City Co	450
Smith Edmund	King William Co	150
Smith ffrancis	King & Queen Co	100
Smith ffrancis	Essex Co	500
Smith George	Northampton Co	133
Smith George	Princess Anne Co	250
Smith Mr Guy	Abbington-Gloucester Co	30
Smith Henry at ye Southerd	owns at Accomack Co	1000
Smith Humphrey	Princess Anne Co	50
Smith Humphrey	Norfolk Co	100
Smith Humphrey	Henrico Co	40
Smith James	Accomack Co	756
Smith James	New Kent Co	80
Smith James	Prince George Co	67
Smith James	Middlesex Co	400
Smith John	" "	700
Smith John Esqr	Abbington-Gloucester Co	2000
Smith John	Essex Co, tax due on	800
Smith John	James City Co	114
Smith John quarter	Essex Co	1000
Smith John	" "	75
Smith John	Petso-Gloucester Co	1300
Smith John, cooper	King & Queen Co	273
Smith John, sawyer	" " "	80
Smith John	Nansemond Co	100
Smith John	Northampton Co	200
Smith John senr	Norfolk Co	1200
Smith John	" "	200
Smith John	" "	127
Smith John	York Co	150
Smith Jonas	Essex Co	100
Smith Joseph	Northampton Co	250
Smith Lawrence	York Co	1700
Smith Nathaniell	New Kent Co	82
Smith Nicholas	Petso-Gloucester Co	280
Smith Nicho! quarter	King & Queen Co	700
Smith Obadiah	Charles City Co	100
Smith Obadiah	owns in Henrico Co	200
Smith Peter	Northampton Co	450
Smith Philip	Ware-Gloucester Co	700
Smith Poplar	Middlesex Co	550
Smith Richard	King & Queen Co	150
Smith Richard	Norfolk Co	600
Smith Richard	Northampton Co	99
Smith Richard, minor	" "	300

		Acres
Smith Richard	Princess Anne Co	200
Smith Richard	Prince George Co	550
Smith Richard	James City Co, tax due Charles City Co	350
Smith Richard	Surry Co	200
Smith Roger	New Kent Co	300
Smith Samuell	Nansemond Co	230
Smith Samuell	Northampton Co	150
Smith Symon	Accomack Co	200
Smith Thomas	" "	300
Smith Thomas of Gingateague	owns in Accomack Co	693
Smith Thomas of Savannah	" " "	200
Smith Thomas	Surry Co	750
Smith Thomas	" "	380
Smith Thomas	Northampton Co, tax due	400
Smith Thomas	Essex Co	50
Smith William for Kittson	Abbington-Gloucester Co	50
Smith William	New Kent Co	110
Smith William	Warwick Co	150
Smith William, quarter	Essex Co	3000
Smith William	" "	150
Smiths in Bristol quarter	King & Queen Co	2800
Smith William	Princess Anne Co	180
Smith William	Isle of Wight Co	2100
Snaill Henry	Princess Anne Co	250
Snead John	New Kent Co	75
Snead Robert	York Co	50
Snead Thomas	New Kent Co	200
Snead Thomas	Essex Co	950
Snell John	King William Co	150
Snelling Elizabeth	Ware-Gloucester Co	250
Snuggs Charles	Henrico Co	400
Soane Capt. Wm	" "	3841
Soane Henry junr	James City Co	750
Sojourner John	Isle of Wight Co	240
Sones Thomas	King & Queen Co	150
Sorrell Mary	James City Co	500
Sorrell Thomas	" " " tax due	300
Sosque Symon	Accomack Co	325
Sott ? Widdo	Northampton Co	750
Southerland Daniell	King & Queen Co	200
Southerland William	" " "	800
Southerne John	Middlesex Co	100
Southworth William	" "	50
Sowel John land, Levingstone on it	King & Queen Co	750
Spaine John	Prince George Co	118
Sparks John	King & Queen Co	200
Sparrow William	Norfolk Co	350
Speares George	Charles City Co	225
Spearman Job	Essex Co	300
Speir Capt. John	Nansemond Co	500
Speirs James	" "	200
Speir Robert	New Kent Co	450
Speirs William	Nansemond Co	200
Spencer Katherine	King & Queen Co	600
Spencer Thomas	" " "	300

		Acres
Spencer Thomas	King William Co	600
Spicer William	Elizabeth City Co	60
Spight Francis	Nansemond Co	400
Spinks John	Ware-Gloucester Co	300
Spiors John	Essex Co	160
Spite William	Nansemond Co	500
Spivey George	" "	200
Spivey James	" "	600
Spivey Matthew	Norfolk Co	600
Spivey Thomas	Nansemond Co	200
Spratt Henry Mr	Princess Anne Co	1736
Spratt Thomas	" " "	600
Sprattley John	James City Co	350
Sprattlin Andrew	New Kent Co	654
Spring Robert	Norfolk Co	98
Spruse Jeremy	King William Co	150
Stafford Mary	James City Co	210
Staice Symon	York Co	200
Stallard Samuell	Essex Co	100
Stalling Elias	Nansemond Co	470
Stallings Elias junr	" "	250
Stallings John	" "	250
Stallings Nicholas	" "	965
Stallings Richard	" "	165
Stamp Ralph	New Kent Co	625
Standard Wm. of Middlesex Co	tax due in King William Co	1000
Standback William	Prince George Co	150
Stanbridge William	Petso-Gloucester Co	159
Stanbro John	Norfolk Co	40
Standley Richard	Norfolk Co	200
Staners Thomas	Essex Co	500
Stanley Edward	Henrico Co	300
Stanley Thomas	New Kent Co	150
Stansell John	Nansemond Co	500
Stanton John	Essex Co	95
Stanton John	Accomack Co	200
Stanup Capt. (Stamp ?)	New Kent Co	1024
Stanup Richard	" " "	325
Stapleton Thomas	King & Queen Co	200
Stapleton Thomas	Middlesex Co	200
Staples William	Nansemond Co	210
Starbridge William	Petso-Gloucester Co	159
Stark John	King William Co	500
Starke Robert	York Co	250
Stark Thomas of London	King & Queen Co (not paid for)	920
Starkey Robert	Abbington-Gloucester Co	100
Starlin Richard	Accomack Co	150
Stear Thomas	York Co	60
Steavens James	Abbington-Gloucester Co	100
Stephens Edward	Petso-Gloucester Co	70
Stephens John	Essex Co	100
Stephens William	New Kent Co	100
Stepp Abraham	Essex Co	390
Stepping Thomas	New Kent Co	350
Sterfarer James	Accomack Co	50
Sterling Capt.	Kingston-Gloucester Co	1100

		Acres
Stevens Charles	Abbington-Gloucester Co	75
Stevens Edward.	" " "	80
Stevens Henry.	" " "	60
Stevenson John	Isle of Wight Co	150
Steward Daniell	Henrico Co	270
Steward John Junr	" "	902
Steward John	Surry Co	200
Sthrashley Thomas	Essex Co	200
Stiff Thomas	Middlesex Co	100
Stith Capt.	Prince George Co	471
Stith Drewry	Charles City Co	1240
Stith John.	" " "	1395
Stoakes John	Abbington-Gloucester Co	300
Stockes John	Charles City Co	476
Stockes Silvanus senr	" " "	250
Stockes Silvanus junr.	" " "	550
Stockley Charles.	Accomack Co	170
Stockley John senr	Northampton Co	370
Stockley Richard.	Surry Co	100
Stockley Thomas	Accomack Co	363
Stocomb Robert	Accomack Co	300
Stogell John	Essex Co	100
Stogsdall Benjamin.	York Co	50
Stokes Henry	Accomack Co	208
Stokes Richard	Essex Co	500
Stokly Christo	Accomack Co	200
Stokley Joseph	" "	664
Stone John	King & Queen Co	295
Stone Mary	" " "	100
Stoner David	York Co	50
Story John	King & Queen Co	3000
Stovell Bartholomew	Henrico Co	100
Stowers Widdo	" "	200
Strange Alexander	New Kent Co	450
Strange John	Essex Co	100
Straton Benjamin.	Northampton Co	745
Streater Edward	Nansemond Co	200
Street Madison.	Isle of Wight Co	150
Street William	King William Co	350
Stringer Hillary	Northampton Co	1250
Stringer Margaret	King & Queen Co	175
Stringer Thomas.	Accomack Co	600
Stringfellow Richard	Surry Co	75
Stroud John	Prince George Co	60
Strukey Charles	Warwick Co	86
Strutton Thomas	King William Co	150
Stubelfield Geo. of Gloucester	owns in King William Co	400
Stubelfield Simon	Ware-Gloucester Co	200
Stubs John	Petso-Gloucester Co	300
Stubbs Susannah	Abbington-Gloucester Co	300
Sturdivant Chichester	Prince George Co	214
Sturdivant Daniell	" " "	850
Sturdivant Matthew	" " "	150
Styles John	New Kent Co	200
Suger John	Surry Co	250
Sugg George	Norfolk Co	408

		Acres
Sugg Joseph	Norfolk Co	300
Sugg William.	" "	200
Sullenger Peter	Essex Co	400
Sullivan Daniell	Nansemond Co	100
Sullivant John	Princess Anne Co	200
Summons John	Surry Co	1300
Sumner Richard	Nansemond Co	600
Sumner Capt. William.	" "	275
Sunter Stephen.	New Kent Co	478
Surly Thomas	King & Queen Co	100
Suthern Henry	Princess Anne Co	640
Sutton William	Middlesex Co	150
Swaine Stephen.	Princess Anne Co	450
Swann Carles	Henrico Co for Col. Randolph	1049
	tax due on land	
Swan Elizabeth.	Isle of Wight Co	600
	tax due Nansemond Co land	
Swann William.	Surry Co	1800
Swinson Richard	King & Queen Co	170
Sworne Thomas Cleaver	Abbington-Gloucester Co	200
(not clear, also placed under Cleaver)		
Sykes Burnard.	James City Co	1012
Sykes Stephen	King & Queen Co	50
Sykes William	Nansemond Co	150
Symmons John	" "	678
Symmons John	" "	100
Symon James.	Norfolk Co	200
Symon Smith	Accomack Co	200
Symons Edward	Petso-Gloucester Co	500
Symons George	New Kent Co	125
Symons Josiah.	" " "	100
Symons Samuell	Warwick Co	173
Symons Thomas	Norfolk Co	166
Symmons Thomas	Prince George Co	566
Symmons William	Princess Anne Co	400
Syrte Elizabeth	Nansemond Co	100

------- T -------

Taburd Michael	Prince George Co	150
Taliaferro Charles.	Essex Co	300
Taliaferro Francis.	" "	1300
Taliaferro John	" "	2000
Talley Henry	Prince George Co	639
Tancock's Orphans	Henrico Co	1230
Tankard William	Northampton Co	450
Tanner Edward	Henrico Co	217
Tanner Paul	Northampton Co	148
Tanner Thomas	Charles City Co	2000
Tapp John.	New Kent Co	110
Tapley Adam	Prince George Co	377
Tapley Sanders.	" " "	300
Tapley Thomas.	" " "	300
Tarendine John.	Charles City Co	150

Acres

Tarte Alice	Norfolk Co	300
Tarte Elezar senr	" "	300
Tarte Elezar junr	" "	595
Tate James	New Kent Co	160
Tatham Edmund	Accomack Co	200
Tatham Nathaniell senr	Prince George Co	501
Tatham Nathaniel junr	" " "	200
Tatham Samuell senr	" " "	100
Tatham Samuell junr	" " "	195
Taverner William	York Co	100
Taylor Andrew	Norfolk Co	222
Taylor Caleb	Nansemond Co	200
Taylor Charles	Accomack Co	580
Taylor Daniell	King & Queen Co	70
Taylor Daniell	York Co	225
Taylor Edward	Accomack Co	300
Taylor Elias	" "	1500
Taylor Ethelred	Surry Co	538
Taylor Jacob	Princess Anne Co	80
Taylor James	Accomack Co	100
Taylor James	King & Queen Co	4000
Taylor James	Prince George Co	306
Taylor Capt. John	" " " (Surry tax on 800 ac)	1700
Taylor James	Kingston-Gloucester Co	50
Taylor John	Prince George Co	100
Taylor John	Norfolk Co	100
Taylor Joseph	New Kent Co	150
Taylor Lemuel	" " "	212
Taylor Richard	Nansemond Co	300
Taylor Richard	" "	300
Taylor Richard	Essex Co	650
Taylor Richard	Norfolk Co	75
Taylor Richard	Surry Co	77
Taylor Robert	Elizabeth City Co	50
Taylor Robert	Accomack Co	95
Taylor Samuell	" "	1232
Taylor Thomas	" "	100
Taylor Thomas	Henrico Co	475
Taylor Thomas	Prince George Co	400
Taylor Thomas	New Kent Co	350
Taylor Thomas	" " "	25
Taylor William	Accomack Co	1400
Taylor William	" "	100
Taylor William	" "	265
Taylor William	York Co	100
Teagle John	Abbington-Gloucester Co	30
Teague Simeon	Northampton Co	100
Teague Thomas	" "	200
Temple William	Prince George Co	100
Ternall Thomas	Accomack Co	150
Terrell Baleaby	Isle of Wight Co	100
Terry James	King William Co	400
Terry Stephen	" " "	330
Terry Thomas	" " "	300
Terseley John	Isle of Wight Co	150

		Acres
Tester Robert	Prince George Co	170
Thacker C. C.	King & Queen Co	1000
Thacker Edwin estate	Middlesex Co	2500
Thacker Henry	" "	1875
Thacker Samuell.	Essex Co	110
Thackson John	James City Co	289
Theobald James	Norfolk Co	140
Theodam John	Elizabeth City Co	100
Thellaball Widdow.	Norfolk Co	600
Thilman Paul	Middlesex Co	300
Thomas Charles.	Nansemond Co	50
Thomas Edward.	York Co	223
Thomas Hanah	James City Co	100
Thomas John.	" " "	250
Thomas John.	Essex Co	100
Thomas John.	Nansemond Co	275
Thomas John junr	" "	100
Thomas Mary	Abbington-Gloucester Co	100
Thomas Mark	Kingston-Gloucester Co	300
Thomasses Orphans.	New Kent Co	500
Thomas Robert quarter	Essex Co	200
Thomas Rowland	King & Queen Co	610
Thomas William	Essex Co	200
Thomas William	James City Co	150
Thomas William	Isle of Wight Co	250
Thompson Capt.	New Kent Co	2600
Thompson James	" " "	100
Thompson Samuell.	Surry Co	3104
Thompson Samuell.	Essex Co	1000
Thompson William.	Nansemond Co	133
Thomson Henry	James City Co	150
Thornhill John	Prince George Co	350
Thornton ffrancis	Essex Co	700
Thornton Francis	Norfolk Co	200
Thornton William senr	Petso-Gloucester Co	525
Thornton William junr.	" " "	800
Thorowgood Adam	Princess Anne Co	700
Thorogood Argoll Mr	" " "	1000
Thorowgood Capt. John	" " "	1000
Thorowgood Robert	" " "	940
Thorp Joseph	Surry Co	250
Thorp Thomas	New Kent Co	200
Thorp Widdo	Essex Co	400
Thorp Thomas (given Throp)	Isle of Wight Co	350
Throgmorton Capt.	Ware-Gloucester Co	500
Throp Thomas	Isle of Wight Co	350
Thrower Alice	Princess Anne Co	125
Thrower Edward	Prince George Co	150
Thrower John	" " "	250
Thrower Thomas	" " "	150
Thurmond Richard	New Kent Co	131
Thurston John	James City Co	500
Thurston Matthew	Norfolk Co	100
Thurston Mrs.	Princess Anne Co	290
Thurston William	Petso-Gloucester Co	200
Thweat James senr	Prince George Co	715

		Acres
Thweat James junr	Prince George Co	100
Tignall John	Warwick Co	392
Tilley Matthew	Essex Co	200
Tillid's Lands	Ware-Gloucester Co	150
Tilliman George	Prince-George Co	446
Tilliman John	" " "	530
Tilney John	Northampton Co	350
Timson William	York Co	1000
Tindall Elizabeth	" "	60
Tinley Elizabeth	Accomack Co	200
Tinsley Cornelius	New Kent Co	220
Tinsley Edward	James City Co	100
Tinsley John	New Kent Co	130
Tinsley Richard	James City Co	100
Tinsley Thomas	Essex Co	111
Tinsley Thomas	New Kent Co	150
Tirrell William	" " "	400
Todd Richard	King & Queen Co	1050
Todd Capt. Thomas	Kingston-Gloucester Co	775
Todd Thomas	Ware-Gloucester Co	884
Todd Thomas quarter	King & Queen Co	2300
Todd Thomas quarter	Essex Co	550
Tomason Thomas	King William Co	150
Tomer John	York Co	335
Tomlin Widdo	Essex Co	400
Tomlin William	" "	1600
Tomlin William	" "	950
Tomlinson William	Prince George Co	400
Tompkins Humphrey	Kingston-Gloucester Co	100
Tompkins Sarah	York Co	250
Tompkins William	Kingston-Gloucester Co	100
Toms William	King William Co	150
Tomson James	James City Co	100
Tony Alexander	New Kent Co	170
Tooke Thomas	Isle of Wight Co	1228
Tooker Major Henry	Surry Co	700
Tooker Major Henry	Prince George Co	181
Tooker Major Henry for ye Merchants in London, Pr. George Co		4600
Tooker Joseph	Prince George Co	200
Tooker Robert	" " "	400
Topladie Robert	York Co	100
Totty Thomas	Henrico Co	260
Toules Henry	Accomack Co	300
Tounson John	" "	200
Tounson Thomas	" "	400
Tounson Thomas Kiquotan	" "	800
Touser Joseph	" "	200
Tovis Edmund	New Kent Co	100
Towland William	Warwick Co	25
Towler Matthew	King William Co	150
Towley John	King & Queen Co	200
Town Elizabeth	New Kent Co	100
Toy Humphrey	Kingston-Gloucester Co	1100
Toy Thomas	King & Queen Co	175
Tozeley Thomas	Middlesex Co	500
Tranter Edward	Princess Anne Co	180

		Acres
Traylor Edward	Henrico Co	100
Traylor William	" "	730
Trent Henry	" "	224
Trevillian John	res ? Tax due Warwick Co	248
Trevit George	Accomack Co	400
Trible Peter	Essex Co	100
Trice James	King & Queen Co	350
Trigoney Henry	Norfolk Co	200
Troneer John	King William Co	100
Trotman Anne	Charles City Co	120
Truett Henry	Accomack Co	240
Tryfort Barth	Northampton Co	147
Trygell William	Isle of Wight Co	100
Tucker Charles	Elizabeth City Co	240
Tucker Elizabeth	Prince George Co	212
Tucker Francis	" " "	100
Tucker Thomas	New Kent Co	700
Tucker Thomas	Elizabeth City Co	60
Tugill Henry	Middlesex Co	200
Tuker John	Norfolk Co	400
Tuker Thomas	" "	280
Tuker Richard	" "	100
Tuker William	" "	100
Tullery Cornelius	res ? Tax due Norfolk Co	150
Tullett John	James City Co	625
Tully James	Princess Anne Co	400
Tully John	Norfolk Co	165
Tully Mark	Princess Anne Co	300
Tully Thomas	" " "	600
Tully William	New Kent Co	200
Tunstall Thomas	King & Queen Co	550
Turberfield Richard	Prince George Co	140
Tureman Ignatius	King & Queen Co	100
Turlington Peter	Accomack Co	79
Turner Edward	" "	750
Turner Edward	Charles City Co	195
Turner Elizabeth	Abbington-Gloucester Co	150
Turner George	Kingston-Gloucester Co	50
Turner George	Essex Co	200
Turner George	New Kent Co	400
Turner George junr	" " "	200
Turner Henry	" " "	250
Turner Henry	Henrico Co	200
Turner Henry	Isle of Wight Co	350
Turner James	New Kent Co	50
Turner Mr. John	Elizabeth City Co	50
Turner John	Isle of Wight Co	950
Turner John	Warwick Co	100
Turner Richard	Northampton Co	50
Turner Richard	King & Queen Co	200
Turner Thomas	" " "	267
Turner William	New Kent Co	250
Turpin Phillip	Henrico Co	444
Turpin Thomas	" "	491
Turpin Thomas	" " tax due 10 acres	100
Turton Thomas	Princess Anne Co	110

Acres

Twine Thomas	James City Co	100
Twitty Thomas	New Kent Co	200
Tyery William	James City Co	1590
Tyler Henry.	" " "	730
Tyler Henry.	York Co	180
Tyler -----?	New Kent Co	100
Tyner Nicholas	Isle of Wight Co	300
Tyrrey Alexander.	New Kent Co	210
Tyrrey James	" " "	150
Tyrey Thomas.	" " "	190
Tyson Matt of Southerd.	Accomack Co (non-res)	300
Tyous Thomas	Surry Co	400

------- U -------

Ubankes Henry	Accomack Co	400
Udall Matthew	James City Co	50
Umpleet William	Elizabeth City Co	25
Underwood Thomas	Isle of Wight Co	100
Upshaw William, quarter	Essex Co	1000
Upshaw William	Petso-Gloucester Co	490
Upsherd John	New Kent Co	60
Upshot Arthur.	Accomack Co	2020
Urvein Nathaniel	Prince George Co	150
Uttley John	King & Queen Co	200

------- V -------

Vadrey Samuell.	Ware-Gloucester Co	400
Vaiding Isaac	James City Co	300
Valine Isaac	Ware-Gloucester Co	100
Valkes Robert.	New Kent Co	500
Vann William	Nansemond Co	100
Vanters Bartho	Essex Co	400
Vasser Peter	Isle of Wight Co	230
Vaughan Cornelius	King & Queen Co	500
Vaughan Daniell	Prince George Co	169
Vaughan Henry	James City Co	1900
Vaughan James	Prince George Co	169
Vaughan John	New Kent Co	250
Vaughan John.	Prince George Co	169
Vaughan Nicholas.	" " "	169
Vaughan Richard	" " "	309
Vaughan Samuell	" " "	169
Vaughan Thomas	Nansemond Co	200
Vaughan Vincent	New Kent Co	410
Vaughan William	" " "	300
Vaughan William	Prince George Co	309
Velle Morriss	Norfolk Co	335
Venables Abraham	New Kent Co	100
Venables John	" " "	200
Ventres Michael	Princess Anne Co	450

		Acres
Verney William	James City Co	50
Vernon Walter	Charles City Co	240
Vernum Lewis	York Co	150
Vibson John	Middlesex Co	100
Vice Amer	New Kent Co	50
Vickery Henry	King William Co	450
Vincent Mary	Surry Co	187
Vincent Vaus	Essex Co	450
Vines Thomas	York Co	200
Vinson Thomas	Prince George Co	550
Virget Job	Essex Co	50
Vize Nathaniell	King & Queen Co	100
Voden Henry	Henrico Co	100

-------- W --------

Wadborn Mich	Norfolk Co	500
Waddill Wm	New Kent Co	375
Waddill Samll	" " "	150
Wade Armiger	York Co	424
Wade Thomas	" "	375
Wades Orphans	Warwick Co	100
Wadlington Paul	King & Queen Co, tax due	150
Wagaman Jacob	Accomack Co	150
Waginer John	Essex Co	400
Wagstaff Bazzill	York Co	127
Waid Edward	James City Co	150
Waid Henry	" " "	150
Waid Thomas	" " "	100
Waid James	New Kent Co	150
Wainhouse Francis	Accomack Co	700
Waite Wm senr	" "	225
Waite Wm junr	" "	600
Waite William	" "	110
Wakefield John	Nansemond Co	50
Wakefield Thomas	" "	150
Wakefield Thomas	Norfolk Co	40
Wakeland William	Essex Co	100
Waldin Samuell	King & Queen Co	275
Walice Thomas	Norfolk Co	150
Walk Thomas	Princess Anne Co	298
Walker Capt	New Kent Co	400
Walker Alex	James City Co	500
Walker Alex junr	James City Co	2025
Walker David	" " "	150
Walker David	" " "	100
Walker George	Princess Anne Co	425
Walker George	Elizabeth City Co	325
Walker James	Accomack Co	525
Walker John	King & Queen Co	6000
Walker John	" " " (for Johnson)	1000
Walker John	Northampton Co	300
Walker Joseph	York Co	615

93

		Acres
Walker Thomas	York Co	100
Walker Thomas	Princess Anne Co	820
Walker Thomas	Abbington-Gloucester Co	300
Walker William	New Kent Co	650
Wall Henry	Prince George Co	275
Wall John	" " "	233
Wall Joseph	Surry Co	150
Wall Joseph junr	" "	150
Wallace Mr. James	Elizabeth City Co	1300
Waller Major John	King William Co	800
Wallis Anthony	Nansemond Co	80
Wallis John	" "	150
Wallis John	Norfolk Co	135
Wallis Richard	" "	250
Wallis William	" "	450
Wallis William	Middlesex Co	300
Wallis William	Prince George Co	200
Wallpoole Richard	" " "	625
Wallsworth William	Princess Anne Co	100
Walstone Henry	" " "	800
Walstone William	Princess Anne Co	400
Walter Elizabeth widdo	Northampton Co	100
Walter John	" "	400
Walthall Henry	Henrico Co	832
Walthall Richard	" "	500
Walthall William	" "	500
Waltham John	Isle of Wight Co	450
Waltham John of Maryland	tax due in Accomack Co on	200
Waltham Peter of New England	" " " "	200
Walton Edward	New Kent Co	450
Walton Edward	" " "	150
Walton Thomas	King & Queen Co	200
Waple John	Surry Co	300
Warberton Thomas	James City Co	190
Ward George	Essex Co	350
Ward James	Nansemond Co	100
Ward John	Norfolk Co	320
Ward Richard	Henrico Co	300
Ward Robert	James City Co	800
Ward Samuell	King & Queen Co	160
Ward Seth	Henrico Co	700
Ward Thomas	Northampton Co	120
Ward Thomas	Surry Co	100
Ward Widdo	Essex Co	200
Ward William	Nansemond Co	200
Ware Edward	King & Queen Co	735
Ware Nicho	" " "	718
Ware Valentine	" " "	487
Waren John	Charles City Co	54
Warren Allen	Surry Co	300
Warren Argoll	Northampton Co	350
Warren James	" "	50
Warren John	" "	525
Warren Joseph	" "	50
Warren Robert	" "	190
Warren Robert	Nansemond Co	100

		Acres
Warren Robert	Surry Co	150
Warren Thomas	" "	1040
Warren William	Princess Anne Co	100
Warrick John	Surry Co	80
Warring Peter	New Kent Co	88
Warington John	Accomack Co	100
Warrington Stephen	" "	400
Wate John	Norfolk Co	400
Waterfield John & Peter	Ware-Gloucester Co	143
Waterfield William	Northampton Co	200
Waters Charles	Ware-Gloucester Co	200
Waters Charles	Kingston-Gloucester Co	100
Waters John	Abbington-Gloucester Co	50
Waters John	Essex Co	150
Waters Richard in Maryland	tax due in Accomack Co	1057
Waters Walter	Isle of Wight Co	150
Waters Walter	Petso-Gloucester Co	200
Waters Lieut-Coll Wm	Northampton Co	700
Waters William	Nansemond Co	600
Waterson Richard	Northampton Co	150
Waterson William	" "	855
Watford Joseph	Norfolk Co	97
Watkins Benjamin	King & Queen Co	60
Watkins Edward	" " "	98
Watkins Edward	Henrico Co	120
Watkins Henry senr	" "	100
Watkins John	Surry Co	1160
Watkins John	Isle of Wight Co	200
Watkins Joseph	Henrico Co	120
Watkins Philip	King & Queen Co	203
Watkins Rebecca	York Co	100
Watkins Richard	Surry Co	1345
Watkins Thomas	Henrico Co	200
Watkins Thomas	Essex Co	400
Watkins Thomas	Norfolk Co	190
Watkins Thomas junr	King & Queen Co	125
Watkins William	" " "	137
Watkins William	New Kent Co	50
Watkins William	Henrico Co	120
Watson David	Accomack Co	200
Watson John senr	Henrico Co	1603
Watson Robert	Accomack Co	425
Watson Robert	Norfolk Co	80
Watson Samuell	Nansemond Co	200
Watson Theophilus	New Kent Co	325
Watts Hugh	Middlesex Co	80
Watts Mr. John	Accomack Co	2450
Watts Matthew	Elizabeth City Co	454
Watts Thomas	King & Queen Co	235
Wayman John	York Co	100
Wead William	Essex Co	200
Weathers Thomas	James City Co	130
Weaver Samuell	New Kent Co	100
Webb Charles	Northampton Co	133
Webb Edward	" "	200
Webb Giles	Henrico Co	7260

		Acres
Webb Henry	Northampton Co	100
Webb Henry	Middlesex Co	100
Webb Isaac	Essex Co	200
Webb James	" "	200
Webb John.	" "	200
Webb John	Henrico Co	100
Webb Mary.	New Kent Co	200
Webb Mary.	Norfolk Co	100
Webb Richard	Nansemond Co	200
Webb Robert	Surry Co	340
Webb Robert	Essex Co	375
Webb Thomas	Accomack Co	50
Webster Joseph	New Kent Co	80
Weeks ffrancis.	Middlesex Co	225
Weeks Widdo.	" "	225
Welburn Mr. Arcado	Accomack Co	1854
Welch Henry	Surry Co	100
Weldey Dorothy	Norfolk Co	25
Weldey George	James City Co	317
Weldon Sarah	" " "	100
Wells Elias.	Warwick Co	50
Wells Elizabeth widdo	" "	155
Wells Emanuel	" "	325
Wells John	York Co	750
Wells Capt. Mills	Warwick Co	425
Wells William.	" "	615
Welsh Edward	Nansemond Co	100
Weshart John	Norfolk Co	150
West Alexander	Accomack Co	550
West Anthony	" "	700
West Giles	New Kent Co	200
West John	Norfolk Co	500
West John junr.	Accomack Co	500
West Coll. John	King William Co	1800
West Mrs. Matilda.	Accomack Co	3600
West Capt. Nathaniel	King William Co	2000
West Nathaniel.	New Kent Co	6370
West Robert	Accomack Co	400
West Capt. Thomas	King William Co	1000
West Thomas	Petso-Gloucester Co	112
West William	Isle of Wight Co	250
West William.	" " "	690
West William.	" " "	50
Westerhouse Adryan senr	Northampton Co	200
Weston Edward.	Norfolk Co	100
Westrah William.	Isle of Wight Co	450
Wetherby Bartho.	Elizabeth City Co	300
Whaley Mary.	James City Co	200
Whaley Mary.	York Co	550
Wharton Elizabeth	Accomack Co	200
Wharton Francis.	" "	600
Wharton John.	" "	150
Wharton John	Princess Anne Co	850
Wharton Thomas	New Kent Co	270
Wheat John Land.	Elizabeth City Co	66
Wheatley Thomas	Isle of Wight Co	400

		Acres
Whedon John junr	Norfolk Co	320
Whedon John junr	" "	100
Whedbey George	" "	200
Whedon William	" "	200
Wheeden Edward	Essex Co	50
Wheeler John	New Kent Co	75
Wheeler Thomas	Essex Co	250
Wheeler William	New Kent Co tax due	150
Wheelis Joseph	King William Co	130
Whett William	Accomack Co	400
Whetton John	" "	90
Whitaker Elizabeth Mrs	Warwick Co	600
Whitaker Henry	" "	60
Whitaker William	James City Co	320
Whitaker William	York Co	1800
Whitbee Robert	King William Co	800
Whitby Nathaniel	Isle of Wight Co	170
Whitby William	Henrico Co	215
White Charles	Surry Co	136
White Chillion	Abbington-Gloucester Co	100
White Chillion	tax due King William Co	300
White George	Nansemond Co	50
White James	Warwick Co	40
White Jerimiah	King & Queen Co	200
White John	New Kent Co	190
White John	" " "	320
White John	Nansemond Co	150
White John	Northampton Co	400
White John	Prince George Co	150
White Joseph	Elizabeth City Co	200
White Joseph	Princess Anne Co	330
White Joseph	York Co	750
White Mrs Mary	Surry Co	200
White Patrick	Princess Anne Co	1250
White Patrick	Norfolk Co	500
White Thomas	King & Queen Co	200
White William	Accomack Co	600
Whitehead Arthur	Isle of Wight Co	250
Whitehead John	King William Co	100
Whitehead Phillip	" " "	3000
Whitehorn Widdo	Essex Co	260
Whithurst James	Princess Anne Co	600
Whithurst Richard	" " "	350
Whithurst Richard	Norfolk Co	150
Whithurst William	" "	150
Whiting Henry	Ware-Gloucester Co	800
Whiting Madm	" " "	950
Whiting Thomas	Petso-Gloucester Co	450
Whitlock John	King William Co	200
Whittmore William	Petso-Gloucester Co	150
Whitworth John	King William Co	200
Whorein John	King & Queen Co	200
Wick Hurldy	Prince George Co	600
Wicker Richard	Princess Anne Co	300
Wickett John	Prince George Co	250
Wickins Seth	Petso-Gloucester Co	50

		Acres
Widdick Henry	Norfolk Co	343
Widgeon Robert	Northampton Co	100
Wiggs Henry	Isle of Wight Co	506
Wiggins Thomas	Nansemond Co	100
Wiggins Thomas	Surry Co	300
Wilbe Owen	Princess Anne Co	100
Wilbourn Thomas	King & Queen Co	250
Wilcock John	Northampton Co	200
Wildbore William	King & Queen Co	100
Wilden Francis	Norfolk Co	100
Wilden Nathaniel	" "	100
Wilder Mich.	" "	200
Wilford Charles	New Kent Co	100
Wilkes Joseph	" " "	250
Wilkins Argoll	Northampton Co	150
Wilkins Francis	Prince George Co	150
Wilkins John	" " "	150
Wilkins John	Northampton Co	150
Wilkins Samuell	James City Co	170
Wilkins Thomas	" " "	600
Wilkins William	Norfolk Co	200
Wilkins William	Prince George Co	900
Wilkinson Henry	Nansemond Co	250
Wilkinson Henry	Isle of Wight Co	350
Wilkinson John	King & Queen Co	100
Wilkinson John	Henrico Co	130
Wilkinson Joseph	" "	76
Wilkinson Matthew	Surry Co	200
Wilkinson Richard	Isle of Wight Co	150
Wilkinson Thomas	Accomack Co	50
Wilkinson William	Isle of Wight Co	200
Will Roger	Surry Co	78
Willeroy Abraham	King William Co	550
Willett Williams	Northampton Co	2650
Willett William	Accomack Co	842
Williams Anne	Isle of Wight Co	150
Williams Charles	Middlesex Co	100
Williams Charles	Surry Co	100
Williams Clerk	New Kent Co	300
Williams Edward	Middlesex Co	100
Williams Elizabeth	King & Queen Co	900
Williams Emanuel	Essex Co	100
Williams George	Prince George Co	210
Williams George	Petso-Gloucester Co	100
Williams Griffith	King William Co	240
Williams Jane	Norfolk Co	400
Williams James	Prince George Co	1436
Williams James	Princess Anne Co	100
Williams John	Essex Co	450
Williams John	Kingston-Gloucester Co	50
Williams John	Isle of Wight Co	600
Williams John	" " "	971
Williams John	King William Co	150
Williams John	King & Queen Co	125
Williams John	Norfolk Co	125
Williams John	" "	200

		Acres
Williams John	York Co	100
Williams Matthew	James City Co	75
Williams Nathaniel.	Accomack Co	64
Williams Phillip	King William Co	100
Williams Robert	Henrico Co	300
Williams Roger	Surry Co	150
Williams Rowlands	Warwick Co	170
Williams Samuell	King William Co	600
Williams Thomas.	Isle of Wight Co	100
Williams Thomas	King & Queen Co	200
Williams Thomas	New Kent Co	100
Williams William	" " "	100
Williams Wm. per himself	Elizabeth City Co	260
Williams Wm. per the school	" " "	600
Williams William	Essex Co	100
Williams William.	Isle of Wight Co	1000
Williams William	" " "	100
Williams William	Surry Co	300
Williamson Bartho	Princess Anne Co	400
Williamson Francis	Isle of Wight Co	2035
Williamson George.	" " "	2735
Williamson John	Essex Co	100
Williamson John	James City Co	120
Williamson John	Norfolk Co	750
Williamson Richard	Princess Anne Co	450
Williamson Robert	Middlesex Co	200
Williamson Thomas	Henrico Co	1077
Williamson Thomas	Essex Co	100
Williamson Valentine	Prince George Co	250
Williamson William	Accomack Co	600
Williamson William	Essex Co	100
Willis Alexander	Princess Anne Co	150
Willis Capt. Francis.	Ware-Gloucester Co	3000
Willis Francis	New Kent Co	134
Willis John senr	Accomack Co	430
Willis John junr	" "	350
Willis John	Norfolk Co	470
Willis Stephen	New Kent Co	500
Willis William	King William Co	250
Wills Thom.	Northampton Co	300
Willoughby Coll. Thomas	Norfolk Co	3200
Willoughby Capt. Thomas	" "	660
Wilmore John	New Kent Co	100
Wilson Benj	King & Queen Co (for	
	Wyats) ld	420
Wilson David	Essex Co	50
Wilson James	New Kent Co	60
Wilson Coll. James	Norfolk Co	2800
Wilson James junr.	" "	200
Wilson John	New Kent Co	200
Willson John senr	Henrico Co	1686
Wilson John junr.	" "	100
Wilson John	Isle of Wight Co	1200
Wilson John	James City Co	140
Wilson Lemuell	Norfolk Co	300
Wilson Thomas	Northampton Co	250

		Acres
Wilson Coll. William	Elizabeth City Co	1024
Wilson William	York Co	50
Wilton Richard	Essex Co	150
Wiltshier Joseph	King & Queen Co	60
Winbourne John	Nansemond Co	400
Winfree Henry	King William Co	300
Winfry Charles	New Kent Co	100
Wingfield Thomas	" " "	150
Winkfield Jarvis	Prince George Co	100
Winkfield Robert	" " "	107
Winkles Richard	" " "	450
Winingham Edward	" " "	100
Winningham John junr	" " "	200
Winningham Thomas	" " "	100
Winslow Henry	Essex Co	100
Winslow Thomas	" "	150
Winsor Wm. (given Minsor)	Elizabeth City Co	150
Winstone Anthony	New Kent Co	310
Winstone Isaac	" " "	850
Winstone Sarah	" " "	275
Winston William	King William Co	170
Wintby Jacob	New Kent Co	250
Winter Timothy	James City Co	250
Winter William	" " "	100
Winter William	Elizabeth City Co	70
Wisdom Francis	Petso-Gloucester Co	150
Wise John senr	Accomack Co	800
Wise John junr	" "	400
Wise Richard	King & Queen Co	209
Wise William	Accomack Co	409
Wise William	York Co	850
Wishart James	Princess Anne Co	225
Wishart William	" " "	200
Witherington Nicholas	Surry Co	100
Withy Thomas	King & Queen Co	50
Wollope Skinner	Accomack Co	2485
Woltham Stephen	" "	244
Woltham Teagle	res. Maryland, Accomack Co tax due	200
Womack Abraham	Henrico Co	560
Womack John	Prince George Co	550
Womack William	Henrico Co	100
Wood Edward	James City Co	300
Wood Edward	Norfolk Co	100
Wood Edward	Princess Anne Co	50
Wood Henry	New Kent Co	100
Wood James	King & Queen Co	800
Wood James	tax due King William Co	500
Wood Matthew	Warwick Co	300
Wood Moses	Henrico Co	100
Wood Patrick	Nansemond Co	200
Wood Richard	James City Co	130
Wood Thomas	" " "	200
Wood Thomas	Essex Co	300
Wood Thomas	Essex Co	50
Wood Thomas	Henrico Co	50

		Acres
Wood Thomas	Isle of Wight Co	50
Wood Thomas	King William Co	300
Wood Thomas	Middlesex Co	70
Wood Walter	New Kent Co	100
Woodall James	" " "	200
Woodam Thomas	Charles City Co	100
Woodfolk Richard	Abbington-Gloucester Co	125
Woodhouse Mr Henry	Princess Anne Co	3000
Woodhouse Horatio	" " "	525
Woodhouse Ruth	" " "	450
Woodhouse William	" " "	300
Wooding Thomas	Norfolk Co	170
Woodland Winifred	Accomack Co	333
Woodley Andrew	Isle of Wight Co	770
Woodley William	Nansemond Co	350
Woodley Robert	Norfolk Co	350
Woodlife Elizabeth	Prince George Co	844
Woodlife John senr	" " "	644
Woodlife John junr	" " "	750
Woodnatt Henry	Essex Co	300
Woodson John	Henrico Co	4060
Woodson Richard	" "	180
Woodson Robert junr	" "	1157
Woodson Widdo	" "	650
Woodson John	New Kent Co	600
Woodward George	James City Co	350
Woodward Henry	Norfolk Co	280
Woodward John	James City Co	650
Woodward Lanslett	" " "	650
Woodward Samuell	" " "	350
Woodward Samuell	Prince George Co	600
Woody James	New Kent Co	130
Woody John	" " "	100
Woody Symon	" " "	50
Woolsey Jacob	King William Co	130
Wooton John	James City Co	150
Wooton Richard	Warwick Co	243
Wootten Thomas	Isle of Wight Co	963
Wooton Thomas	York Co	150
Worden James	Norfolk Co	200
Worminton John	" "	200
Wormley Esqr. Estate	Middlesex Co	5200
Wormley Madam quarter	King William Co	3000
Worrell Joseph	Nansemond Co	270
Worrin Robert	New Kent Co	300
Worrinton George	Princess Anne Co	400
Worsham John	Henrico Co	1104
Wortham Charles	" "	90
Wortham George	" "	400
Wortham George	Middlesex Co	400
Worthern Richard	Prince George Co	1600
Wotham Jane	Petso-Gloucester Co	60
Wragg Thomas	James City Co	500
Wright James	Norfolk Co	216
Wright Capt. John	Res ? Nansemond Co tax due	?
Wright John	York Co	100

		Acres
Wright Mary	James City Co	175
Wright Mary	Accomack Co	200
Wright Samuell	James City Co	100
Wright Thomas	King William Co	150
Wright Thomas	King & Queen Co	300
Wright Thomas	Surry Co	100
Wright William	Norfolk Co	574
Wyatt Alice	New Kent Co	1300
Wyatt Anthony	Prince George Co	250
Wyatt Conquest	Petso-Gloucester Co	2200
Wyatt John	King & Queen Co	530
Wyatt Capt. Nich.	Prince George Co	700
Wyatt Richard	King & Queen Co	1843
Wyatt Richard	Essex Co & John Pettus, tax due	800
Wyatt Widdo	Charles City Co	800
Wyth John	York Co	100
Wyth Capt. Joseph	Prince George Co	860
Wynn Richard	Nansemond Co	890
Wynn Capt. Thomas	Prince George Co	400

------- Y -------

Yancey Charles	King William Co	100
Yarborough John	" " "	150
Yarborough Richard	" " "	300
Yarborrow Robert	Abbington-Gloucester Co	100
Yard Robert	Petso-Gloucester Co	450
Yates John	Nansemond Co	400
Yates Robert	" "	150
Yeoell Judith	New Kent Co	150
Yeoman John	" " "	50
Yorgen Widdow	Warwick Co	60
York Matthew	King & Queen Co	100
Young Dorrell	Prince George Co	383
Young Edward	York Co	100
Young Giles	Accomack Co	100
Young Giles	Essex Co	100
Young John	Surry Co	300
Young John	Elizabeth City Co	440
by Robert Charwill for J. Young.		
Young John	Prince George Co	200
Young Robert	James City Co	350
Young Samuell	Accomack Co	50
Young Thomas	James City Co	350
Young William	Accomack Co	144
Young William	Essex Co	1000

"The preceeding Sheets are true copys of the Rent Rolls for the year 1704 given in and accounted for by the several Sherifs in April 1905 and sworne to before his Excellency according to wch they made up their accots of the Quit Rents with

Wil Robertson Cl. Con.

LAND GRANTS

by the

PROPRIETORS

of the

NORTHERN NECK OF VIRGINIA

103

Grants By the Proprietors of the Northern Neck in Virginia

------- A -------

Acres

Adams John	1705	Stafford Co	393
Adington Susanna, wid. of Benj	1692	Westmoreland Co	103
Ailiff Richard	1704	Stafford Co	370-456
Allen William	1708	" "	148
Allerton Isaac	1690/4	" "	1000-1050
Allerton Isaac	1690/4	Westmoreland Co.	64-248-1950
Andrews Robert	1692	Westmoreland Co	576
Angell Huriah	1695	Lancaster Co	212
Ashbury Henry	1704	Westmoreland Co	80
Austin James	1694	Northumberland Co	284
Ayliff Richard	1706	Stafford Co	456

------- B -------

Bach Peter	1694	Stafford Co	400
Bacheller Thomas	1704	Westmoreland Co	151
Baile Peter	1694	Stafford Co	400
Baker Samuel	1694	Westmoreland Co	154
Bale William	1698	Lancaster Co	172
Ball John	1699	Stafford Co	300
Ball Gerald & Robert	1708	Westmoreland Co	200
Ball Lt. Col. Joseph	1704	Lancaster Co	80
Ball Robert & Gerald.	1708	Westmoreland Co	200
Ball Capt. William	1706	Richmond Co	1093
Barber Capt. Charles	1708	" "	85
Barber Capt. William	1708	Stafford Co	400-800
Barker Thomas	1708	Lancaster Co	102
Barber William	1703	Stafford Co	400
Barnard Elizabeth	1695	" "	150
Barton Thomas	1697	" "	100
Batting Nicholas	1696	" "	547
Baxter Thomas	1703	" "	1907
Baysey Edmund	1704	Northumberland Co	157
Beard Andrew	1694	Westmoreland Co	107
Belfield Joseph.	1704	Richmond Co	555
Bennett John & Vincent Cox	1709	Westmoreland Co	765
Bennett William	1708	Stafford Co	291
Berry William & Sem Cox	1704	Richmond Co	349
for Berryman see Bury-			
Bertrand John clerk	1698	Lancaster Co	924
Betts Charles	1694	Northumberland Co	115
Boatman Henry	1695	Lancaster Co	250
Boatman Henry.	1706	" "	52
Brent George & Wm. Fitzhugh.	1690	Stafford Co	?
Brent George of Woodstock	1691	" "	1248
Brent George	1692/4	" "	1050-200-50-1543

			Acres
Brent George	1694/5	Stafford Co	567-1395
Brent George	1694/5	" "	1385
Brent George	1694	Westmoreland Co	1050
Brent Henry	1694	" "	1200
Brent Nicholas	1691	Stafford Co	1700
Brent Robert	1694	Westmoreland Co	500
Bridges William	1690	" "	700
Bristow Robert	1697	Lancaster Co	90
Broadland Thomas	1705/6	Stafford Co	283
Brooks Thomas	1704	Richmond & Stafford	322-322
Brooks Thomas & Ed. Mountjoy	1709	Richmond Co	800
Brown David	1704	Westmoreland Co	440
Brown David & Samuel Read "part of record states Daniel	1695	Westmoreland Co	590
Brown George	1694 & 1706	Westmoreland	324-186
Brown John	1694	Westmoreland Co	100
Brown Thom. & George	1709	" "	130
Brown William	1709	Richmond Co	38
Brown Wm. & Richard Sutton	1707	Westmoreland Co	1799
Brush William	1709	Lancaster Co	50
Bryan John	1695	Northumberland Co	300
Bryant Richard & John Rowley	1690	Stafford Co	385
Bryan Thomas junr	1709	Richmond Co	167
Buckner Philip	1692	Stafford Co	90
Buckner Richard	1709	Richmond Co	20
Bunbury John & William	1691	Stafford Co	640
Burberry Malachi	1704	Northumberland Co	136
Burkett John & Wm. Pennell	1708	Richmond Co	300
Buryman Benjamin	1699	Westmoreland Co	60
Bushrod Ann	1700 & 1704	Northumberland	39-26
Bushrod John	1709	Westmoreland Co	88
Butler Peter	1696	Richmond Co	350
Butler Thomas	1707	Westmoreland Co	157

------- C -------

Calmeby Marquis	1706	Stafford Co	744-711
Calvert Charles	1705	" "	200
Calvert Sarah & Ann	1705	" "	219
Carpenter Anthony	1707	Westmoreland Co	164
Carpenter Richard	1698	Stafford Co	167
Carr Joseph	1709	" "	326
Carter Charles	1709	Richmond Co	77-1100-242
Carter Robert junr	1707	Stafford Co	912
Carter William	1694	Richmond Co	89
Champ John	1694	Stafford Co	340
Champion John	1691	Northumberland Co	176
Chapman Thomas	1694	Stafford Co	443
Chapples Henry	1694	Richmond Co	100
Church Thomas	1694	Stafford Co	124
Churchill Samuel	1704	Richmond Co	344

Acres

Claitor Thomas	1691/2	Westmoreland Co	152
Clarke Maurice	1710	Richmond Co	150
Clerk Robert	1704	" "	1954
Cole Robert	1705	Westmoreland Co	180
Coleclough Benjamin	1694	Stafford Co	150
Coleston William	1694	Richmond Co	100
Collingsworth John & Thom	1691	Westmoreland Co	200
Collingsworth from Pierce	1691	" "	200
Combs William	1705	Richmond Co	200
Conway Dennis	1703/4	Northumberland Co	110
Conyers Henry	1706	Stafford Co	233
Cooke John	1697	Northumberland Co	50
Coppidge William	1705	" "	187
Cornhill John Innis	1698	Westmoreland Co	197
Cornish William	1705	Northumberland Co	262
Coward James	1709	Richmond Co	121
Cox Sem	1694/5	" "	378
Cox Sem & Wm. Berry	1704	" "	349
Cox Sem	1694/5	Stafford Co	378
Cox Vincent & John Bennett	1709	Westmoreland Co	765
Crosby Daniel	1710	Stafford Co	262
Crosby George	1708	" "	122
Crosswell Gilbert & John Jones	1697	Richmond Co	139
Crosswell and Jones	1699	Westmoreland Co	139
Crouch John	1709	Stafford Co	200
Cursonwell Francis	1695	Northumberland Co	100
Curtis John	1703	Lancaster Co	800

------- D -------

Darrell Sampson	1694	Stafford Co	200
Davis John	1694	Westmoreland Co	50
Dawson Henry	1697-1700	Northumberland	99-225
Derrick Thom. & Sam Wells	1694	Stafford Co	363
Dew Andrew	1708	Richmond Co	302
Dike Matt & Edw. Ford	1692	Stafford Co	1344
Downing George	1704	Northumberland Co	70
Downing Thomas	1704	" "	646
Downing Capt. William	1692/1703	Stafford Co	770-200
Downing William	1694	Stafford Co	228
Dunnahaw Hugh	1706	Westmoreland Co	48
Duncan Henry	1704	" "	197
Dymert Elizabeth	1697	Lancaster Co	1300

------- E -------

Edwards John	1694	Westmoreland Co	197
Edwards Meredith	1694	" "	150
Ellis Peter	1706	" "	118
Eskridge George	1704/8/9	" "	58-305
Evan Thomas	1694	Richmond Co	110

------- F -------

		Acres
Farlow Ambrose	1704 Stafford Co	150
Farrow Abraham	1694/5-1704 Stafford Co	400-800-550
Farrow Abraham with Capt. Tho. Harrison	1708 Stafford Co	880
Fields Daniel	1703 Stafford Co	1128
Fields Daniel, wife Mary	1704 Westmoreland Co	150
Fields Daniel	1707 Stafford Co	298
Fisher Martin.	1691/2 Westmoreland Co	726
Fitzgarrick Dan & Edw. Merrick .	1707 " "	280
Fitzhugh Henry	1707 Stafford Co	951
Fitzhugh Colonel	1690 " "	200-150-300
Fitzhugh Wm. & George Brent. . .	1690 " "	?
Fitzhugh Wm. & John Newton. . . .	1690 " "	500-550-2150
Fitzhugh William	1694 " "	800-1600-21996
Fitzhugh William	1694/5/6 Westmoreland Co	2672
Fitzhugh William	1695/6 Richmond Co	350
Fitzhugh William	1696 Westmoreland Co	2197
Flint Richard.	1694 Lancaster Co	150
Foot Richard	1708 Stafford Co	204
Ford Edward & Matthew Dike. . . .	1692 " "	1344
Forster Robert.	1691 Westmoreland Co	185
Fossaker Rich. & Wm. Waller. . .	1692 Stafford Co	400-800
Fowler Richard	1704 Richmond Co	230
Fox David	1694 Lancaster Co	128-200-420
Franke Robert.	1694 Westmoreland Co	335
Frankline Edw. & Robt. Sandford .	1692 " "	413
Fox William	1704 Lancaster Co	178
Fryar John	1694 Westmoreland Co	100

------- G -------

		Acres
Gallop Henry	1709 Richmond Co	109
Gardner John junr.	1700 Westmoreland Co	200
Garland Nathaniel.	1692 " "	205
Garland Thomas	1692 " "	81
Garner John	1709 " "	180-390
Garner John	1707 Northumberland Co	36
Garner Parish	1709 " "	92
Gaylord Mrs Ann	1690 " "	500
Gaylord Mrs relict and widow of James Gaylord		
George William	1694 Lancaster Co	81
Gibson Richard	1694 Stafford Co	26
Giles Traverse	1708 " "	22
Gill Thomas	1705 Northumberland Co	138
Glass-cock George	1707 Richmond Co	45
Goade Abraham	1704 " "	208
Goin Thomas	1708 Stafford Co	653
Gosling John	1708-1691 Stafford Co	566-400
Goury John	1706 Stafford Co	129
Green George.	1708 Richmond Co	885

			Acres
Greenhouse William	1694 Stafford Co		200
Gregg James	1707 " "		240
Gregg Thomas junr.	1694/5/8 Stafford Co		200-795
Griffie Lewis	1704 Richmond Co		414
Griffen Lewis	1694/5 Stafford Co		154
Griffen Thomas	1707 Richmond Co		3471
Grigsby John	1709 Stafford Co		887
Gullick Thomas	1694 Westmoreland Co		234
Gilson Tho. & Rice Hooe	1694 Stafford Co		1100

------- H -------

Hack George Nicholson.	1695 Stafford Co		1100
Haines James	1694 Lancaster Co		250
Halley Henry	1704 " "		
Hamersley Francis			
Hammock William	1694 Richmond Co		300
Hammock William	1697/99 Westmoreland Co		
			161-214
Hammon Peter	1694 Northumberland Co		
Hanie Anthony	1707 " "		75
Hanxford John	1704 Richmond Co		77-100
Hardwicke James	1697 Westmoreland Co		200
Harney John	1695/6 Stafford Co		234
Harnis Edward	1694 Westmoreland Co		200
Harris John	1694 Northumberland Co		150
Harris John & John Haynie sr . . .	1694 " "		200
Harris John	1695 " "		200
Harris with John Turberville. . . .	1695 " "		
Harris Wm & Lewis Markham . . .	1690 Stafford Co		1600
Harris William	1691 " "		383
Harrison Burr	1698 " "		100- 200
Harrison George	1697 Westmoreland Co		354
Harrison Robert	1708 Richmond Co		218
Harrison Capt. Thomas & William	1707 Stafford Co		294
Harrison with Abraham Farrow . .	1708 " "		880
Harrison with Thom Walter	1705 " "		112
Harrison with Pearson group . . .	1706 " "		4639
Hart Edwd. & wife Margaret	1690 Westmoreland Co		880
Hartley John	1697 Richmond Co		649
Hartley John	1697 Westmoreland Co		699
Harvey James	1709 Stafford Co		600
Harvey Thomas.	1697 Stafford Co		220
Harvey Thomas.	1697 Richmond Co		220
Harvey Thomas.	1697 Westmoreland Co		220
Harwell Richard	1695 Lancaster Co		160
Haydon Thomas	1695 Northumberland Co		100
Haynes James	1695/6 Lancaster Co		208-250
Haynie John senr.	1694 Northumberland Co		100
Haynie with John Harris	1694 " "		200
Hayword Samuel	1694 Stafford Co		1050
Headges Robert.	1708 " "		160-346
Heals George	1692 Lancaster Co		350
Henson Joseph	1694 Stafford Co		195

			Acres
Hewgate James	1707	Westmoreland Co	144
Hewlett John	1695	Northumberland Co	300
Hewes Richard	1700	" "	161
Higgins Augustine & John	1706	Richmond Co	110
Hill John	1705	Northumberland Co	300
Hill John	1707	" "	250
Hoar John	1707	Westmoreland Co	20
Hobson Thomas	1705	Northumberland Co	600
Hogan John	1710	Stafford Co	740
Hooe Rice & Tho. Gilson	1694	" "	1100
Hooe Col. Rice senr	1704	" "	200-558
Hooe Rice jr & Col. Rice Hooe	1704	" "	200
Hoopper Thomas	1708-10	"	1614-900
Hooper Thomas	1708	" "	489-1614
Hornbuckle Elinor	1708	Westmoreland Co	200
Hornsby Mary	1706	Northumberland Co	93- 27
Howson John	1704	" "	364
Hudnell Partain	1695	" "	150
Hudson John	1704	Westmoreland Co	70
Hudson Jos hua	1704	" "	100
Huggett Michael	1692	Richmond Co	142
land escheates goes to Co. Justices of the Peace.			
Hughes Richard (given as Hewes)	1700	Northumberland Co	161
Humstone Edward	1705	Stafford Co	200-489
Hunt Francis	1703	" "	50-50

------- I -------

Indigo John & James	1704	Richmond Co	307
Innis James	1703/4	" "	628
Innis James	1704	" "	975-624
Innis James	1704/11	" "	104-128-333

------- J -------

Jackson Andrew	1704	Richmond Co	908-1238
Jackson Samuel	1694	Stafford Co	450
Jacob John	1695	Richmond Co	218
James Thomas	1699	Stafford Co	100
Jenkins Walter	1694	Northumberland Co	500
Jones James	1703/4	" "	50-647
Jones John	1697	Richmond Co	139
Jones with Gilbert Croswell		" "	
Jones with Gilbert Croswell	1699	Westmoreland Co	139
Jones Roderick	1692	Richmond Co	200
Jones Capt. William	1704	Northumberland Co	236
Jones Capt. William	1705	" "	200
Jones Capt. Wm.	1706	" "	245

------- K -------

			Acres
Keen John	1709	Northumberland Co	81
Kelley John	1704	Stafford Co	50
Kelley Wilford	1704	" "	50
Kent Samuel	1691/2	" "	344
Kill Charles	1694	Richmond Co	87-355
King Joseph	1705	Stafford Co	185-358
King Joseph	1706	" "	338
Kirk Christopher	1703/4	Lancaster Co	100
Kirk Henry	1697	Westmoreland Co	100
Kneaton Augustine	1694	Stafford Co	327-104
Knight Thomas	1704	Richmond Co	1250
Knight Thomas	1705	Northumberland Co	60-80
Koherin William	1698	Westmoreland Co	100
Kyrbey John	1691	Lancaster Co	200
Kyrton Thomas	1690	Stafford Co	600

------- L -------

Lampkin James	1707	Westmoreland Co	464
Lampkin with Robert Phillips		" "	
Lancaster John	1695/6	Northumberland Co	140
Landman John	1694	Richmond Co	1683
Lawson Rowland	1699	Lancaster Co	24
Leachman Tho. & W. Williams	1710	Stafford Co	632
Leather John	1709	Lancaster Co	50
Lee Hancock	1704	Richmond Co	1750-1353
Lee Hancock	1705	" "	1100-470
Lee Hancock	1705/7	" "	460-460-1025
Lennis Robert	1704	Lancaster Co	50
Loyde Col. William	1690	" "	300
Lewis John	1695	Northumberland Co	150
Lewis Thom. & Edward Lewis	1690	" "	528
Lewis Thom. & Edward Lewis	1691	" "	360
Lewis Thom with Wm. Morgan	1691	" "	
Lilly John	1706	Stafford Co	124
Lincoln John	1697	Richmond Co	114
Littlejohn Oliver	1707	Lancaster Co	42
Long Henry	1706	Richmond Co	162
Long Josias	1994	Northumberland Co	150
Lord Mrs. Elizabeth	1691	Westmoreland Co	300
Loyd John	1708	Richmond Co	385
Loyde Col. William	1690	Lancaster Co	300
Ludwell Phillip	1709	Richmond Co	2020-3840
Lund Thomas	1703	Stafford Co	470-250-1100
Lunsford James	1705/6	" "	129
Lyne Thomas	1707	Lancaster Co	42

------- M -------

------- N -------

111

			Acres
Onsley Thomas............	1694	Stafford Co	150-1000
Omohundro Richard	1695	Westmoreland Co	282

------- P -------

Paise Thomas............	1707	Richmond Co	320
Payne William	1690	Westmoreland Co	40
Peale Malachi	1694	Stafford Co	1614
Pearson Thomas & John West	1706	" "	660
Pearson with Wm & Tho. Harrison	1706	" "	4639
Pennell Thomas...........	1705	Richmond Co	135
Pennell William	1706	" "	45
Pennell with John Burkett	1708	" "	300
Phillips James	1698	Lancaster Co	200
Phillips Robert	1707	Westmoreland Co	464
Pooll Thomas	1694	Stafford Co	365
Pope John.............	1709	" "	2681
Pope Lawrence	1703	Westmoreland Co	376
Pope Nathaniel	1699/0	Richmond Co	117
Pope Nathaniel with ----- Bridges	1699/0	" "	404
Porte Robert............	1703	Richmond Co	430
Porter Edward...........	1704	Westmoreland Co	119
Powell John	1696	Richmond Co	1696
Pratt John.............	1704	Stafford Co	183

------- R -------

Ramsey Moses	1709	Stafford Co	500
Ransdell Edward	1706	Westmoreland Co	141
Rankin John	1694	Richmond Co	32
Read Samuel	1694/5	Westmoreland Co	590
Read with David or Daniel Brown ..		" "	
Reamy William	1698	" "	123
Reynolds Wm & John	1697	Richmond Co	500
Rice John	1691	Westmoreland Co	100
Ridgewell Richard	1710	Stafford Co	166
Robinson John	1694	Northumberland Co	241
Robinson Major William	1707	Richmond Co	3036
Roe Bunce	1692	Westmoreland Co	163-331
Rogers James	1707	Northumberland Co	100
Roub Thomas	1706	Richmond Co	120
Rowley John	1690	Stafford Co	200
Rowley with Richard Bryant	1690	" "	385
Rush William	1704	Westmoreland Co	100
Russell Rich. wife Hannah	1706	Northumberland Co	400

------- S -------

			Acres
Salisbury Andrew	1696	Northumberland Co	300
Sanford Robert	1699	Westmoreland Co	16
Sanford with Edw. Frankline	1692	" "	413
Sandiford Thomas	1703-09	Stafford Co	105-589
Scarlett Capt. Martin	1691/2	" "	320
Seddon Thomas	1709	" "	229
Self Francis	1708	Northumberland Co	100
Self Stephen	1707	Westmoreland Co	100
Shaw John	1695	Lancaster Co	50
Sherwood William	1696	Stafford Co	2109
Shinroe John	1694	Westmoreland Co	70
Simons John	1703	Richmond Co	116
Simpson John	1698	Stafford Co	100
Simson John	1694/5	" "	627
Singleton Robert	1705	" "	600
Smithe Charles	1699	Westmoreland Co	133
Smith John	1705	Richmond Co	392
Smith Capt. John	1690	Northumberland Co	1200
Smith John	1709	" "	75-392
Smith Peter junr	1692	Westmoreland Co	70
Smith Richard	1692	Northumberland Co	400
Smith William	1694	Richmond Co	84-320
Smoot William senr	1700	" "	262
Smoot William	1704	Westmoreland Co	300
Smoot William	1704	Richmond Co	409
Spence Alexander	1694	" "	47
Spence Patrick	1706	Westmoreland Co	63
Spencer John	1690	" "	820
Spry John	1705/6	Stafford Co	117
Spry John	1709	Northumberland Co	67
Stewart William	1705	Richmond Co	133
Story James	1704/5	" "	32-441
Story John	1694	Stafford Co	150
Stott Bryan	1703/4	Lancaster Co	70
Stott John	1704	Lancaster Co	55
Strutfield Wm	1704/9	Stafford Co	500-534
Sumner Joseph	1691	" "	1800
Sutton Rich. & Wm. Brown	1707	Westmoreland Co	92
Swan Alexander	1694/5	Richmond Co	78-128
Swan Alexander	1704	Lancaster Co	150
Swan Alexander	1704	Richmond Co	190-1200
Symons John	1705	" "	130

------- T -------

Tanner Thomas	1691/2	Westmoreland Co	500
Tarpley Capt. John	1704	Richmond Co	180-100
Taylor Edward	1703	" "	83
Taylor John Wright	1697	Westmoreland Co	229
Taylor John & Thomas	1704	Northumberland Co	1668
Taylor Lazarus	1704	" "	660

			Acres
Taylor Thomas & John	1704	Northumberland Co	1668
Tebbs Daniel and Daniel Tebbs	1703/4	Richmond Co	1350
Thomas Evan	1694	" "	110
Thomas James	1707	" "	729
Thompson Thomas	1703/4	Westmoreland Co	53
Thompson William	1695/6	" "	85
Thorne George	1694	" "	152
Tibbett Thomas	1707	Richmond Co	37
Tillett Giles	1706	Stafford Co	198
Tucker John	1698	Westmoreland Co	165
Turberville John & John Harris	1695	Northumberland Co	200
Turberville John	1705	Richmond Co	78-798
Turberville John	1704	Lancaster Co	78

------- V -------

Vandegasteel Giles	1694	Stafford Co	420
Vicaris Martha	1703	Richmond Co	1260

------- W -------

Waddington Francis	1694	Stafford Co	500
Waddington John	1709	Northumberland Co	99
Waddington Geo. & Robert	1694	" "	200
Waddington Robert & Geo	1694	" "	200
Waddy Thomas	1704	" "	310
Walker Ralph	1694	Stafford Co	1150
Wallor Wm. & Rich Fossaker	1694	" "	800-400
Wallis John	1698	" "	150
Wallis Thomas	1694/5	" "	369
Walter Thom & Edw. Mountjoy	1703/4	Richmond Co	931
Walter with Tho. Harrison	1704	Stafford Co	112
Walter Thomas	1704	" "	1352
Walters Ann	1694	" "	200
Washington John	1692	Westmoreland Co	300
Washington Laurence Capt.	1691-96	" "	25-550
Waters Thomas	1705	Northumberland Co	90
Waugh David	1710	Stafford Co	600
Waugh John	1691/2/4/5		220-6350
Waugh John junr	1706	Stafford Co	298
Waugh John	1709	" "	
		525-1025 ac(1710)	-3402
Weedon Benj & Charles	1695	Westmoreland Co	169
Weedon George	1694	" "	236
Wells John	1692	Lancaster Co	153
Wells Samuel & Tho. Derrick	1694	Westmoreland Co	363
West John senr	1703	Stafford Co	100
West with Pearson group	1706	" "	4639
Wharton Elizabeth	1706	Westmoreland Co	100
Wheeler John	1694	" "	64
White Daniel	1694	" "	292
White Phillip	1694	" "	100

Acres

White Thomas	1708 Richmond Co		51
Whitehead Richard	1694 Stafford Co		393
Whitson Joseph	1694 " "		300
Wigginton William	1694 " "		85
Wildy William	1704/5 Northumberland Co		
			102-216
Williams John	1698 Westmoreland Co		28
Williams Rice	1691/2 " "		107
Williams Thomas	1691 Northumberland Co		500
Williams William	1694 Stafford Co	106-186-589	
Williams William with Tho. Leachman	1710 " "		632
Willis Richard	1691 Lancaster Co		92-296
Wood William	1705 Richmond Co		500
Woods John	1695/6 Stafford Co		2960
Wright John	1707 Westmoreland Co		61
Wright John	1691 " "		107-250
Wright Matrum	1698 Lancaster Co		573

------- Y -------

Young Bryan	1706 Stafford Co	365